ISBN 0-8373-1057-1

C-1057   CAREER EXAMINATION SERIES

This is your PASSBOOK® for...

Emergency Complaint Operator

Test Preparation Study Guide

Questions & Answers

NATIONAL LEARNING CORPORATION

(516) 921-8888
(800) 645-6337
FAX: (516) 921-8743
www.passbooks.com
sales @ passbooks.com
info @ passbooks.com

PRINTED IN THE UNITED STATES OF AMERICA

PASSBOOK®

NOTICE

PASSBOOK® SERIES

THE *PASSBOOK® SERIES* has been created to prepare applicants and candidates for the ultimate academic battlefield — the examination room.

At some time in our lives, each and every one of us may be required to take an examination — for validation, matriculation, admission, qualification, registration, certification, or licensure.

Based on the assumption that every applicant or candidate has met the basic formal educational standards, has taken the required number of courses, and read the necessary texts, the *PASSBOOK® SERIES* furnishes the one special preparation which may assure passing with confidence, instead of failing with insecurity. Examination questions — together with answers — are furnished as the basic vehicle for study so that the mysteries of the examination and its compounding difficulties may be eliminated or diminished by a sure method.

This book is meant to help you pass your examination provided that you qualify and are serious in your objective.

The entire field is reviewed through the huge store of content information which is succinctly presented through a provocative and challenging approach — the question-and-answer method.

A climate of success is established by furnishing the correct answers at the end of each test.

You soon learn to recognize types of questions, forms of questions, and patterns of questioning. You may even begin to anticipate expected outcomes.

You perceive that many questions are repeated or adapted so that you can gain acute insights, which may enable you to score many sure points.

You learn how to confront new questions, or types of questions, and to attack them confidently and work out the correct answers.

You note objectives and emphases, and recognize pitfalls and dangers, so that you may make positive educational adjustments.

Moreover, you are kept fully informed in relation to new concepts, methods, practices, and directions in the field.

You discover that you are actually taking the examination all the time: you are preparing for the examination by "taking" an examination, not by reading extraneous and/or supererogatory textbooks.

In short, this PASSBOOK®, used directedly, should be an important factor in helping you to pass your test.

EMERGENCY COMPLAINT OPERATOR

DUTIES
Answers 911 emergency calls in a central police communications bureau; ascertains essential information from complainant such as name, location and nature of complaint. Relays calls by typing data into a computer-aided dispatch system or by printing on a message card. Work is performed in accordance with standard police procedures, and is supervised by a supervising officer of the police department. Does related work as required.

SCOPE OF THE EXAMINATION
The <u>written test</u> will cover knowledge, skills and/or abilities in such areas as:

1. Retaining and comprehending spoken information from calls for emergency services;
2. Understanding and interpreting written material;
3. Coding/decoding information;
4. Name and number checking; and
5. Map reading.

HOW TO TAKE A TEST

I. YOU MUST PASS AN EXAMINATION

A. WHAT EVERY CANDIDATE SHOULD KNOW

Examination applicants often ask us for help in preparing for the written test. What can I study in advance? What kinds of questions will be asked? How will the test be given? How will the papers be graded?

As an applicant for a civil service examination, you may be wondering about some of these things. Our purpose here is to suggest effective methods of advance study and to describe civil service examinations.

Your chances for success on this examination can be increased if you know how to prepare. Those "pre-examination jitters" can be reduced if you know what to expect. You can even experience an adventure in good citizenship if you know why civil service exams are given.

B. WHY ARE CIVIL SERVICE EXAMINATIONS GIVEN?

Civil service examinations are important to you in two ways. As a citizen, you want public jobs filled by employees who know how to do their work. As a job seeker, you want a fair chance to compete for that job on an equal footing with other candidates. The best-known means of accomplishing this two-fold goal is the competitive examination.

Exams are widely publicized throughout the nation. They may be administered for jobs in federal, state, city, municipal, town or village governments or agencies.

Any citizen may apply, with some limitations, such as the age or residence of applicants. Your experience and education may be reviewed to see whether you meet the requirements for the particular examination. When these requirements exist, they are reasonable and applied consistently to all applicants. Thus, a competitive examination may cause you some uneasiness now, but it is your privilege and safeguard.

C. HOW ARE CIVIL SERVICE EXAMS DEVELOPED?

Examinations are carefully written by trained technicians who are specialists in the field known as "psychological measurement," in consultation with recognized authorities in the field of work that the test will cover. These experts recommend the subject matter areas or skills to be tested; only those knowledges or skills important to your success on the job are included. The most reliable books and source materials available are used as references. Together, the experts and technicians judge the difficulty level of the questions.

Test technicians know how to phrase questions so that the problem is clearly stated. Their ethics do not permit "trick" or "catch" questions. Questions may have been tried out on sample groups, or subjected to statistical analysis, to determine their usefulness.

Written tests are often used in combination with performance tests, ratings of training and experience, and oral interviews. All of these measures combine to form the best-known means of finding the right person for the right job.

II. HOW TO PASS THE WRITTEN TEST

A. NATURE OF THE EXAMINATION

To prepare intelligently for civil service examinations, you should know how they differ from school examinations you have taken. In school you were assigned certain definite pages to read or subjects to cover. The examination questions were quite detailed and usually emphasized memory. Civil service exams, on the other hand, try to discover your present ability to perform the duties of a position, plus your potentiality to learn these duties. In other words, a civil service exam attempts to predict how successful you will be. Questions cover such a broad area that they cannot be as minute and detailed as school exam questions.

In the public service similar kinds of work, or positions, are grouped together in one "class." This process is known as *position-classification*. All the positions in a class are paid according to the salary range for that class. One class title covers all of these positions, and they are all tested by the same examination.

B. FOUR BASIC STEPS

1) Study the announcement

How, then, can you know what subjects to study? Our best answer is: "Learn as much as possible about the class of positions for which you've applied." The exam will test the knowledge, skills and abilities needed to do the work.

Your most valuable source of information about the position you want is the official exam announcement. This announcement lists the training and experience qualifications. Check these standards and apply only if you come reasonably close to meeting them.

The brief description of the position in the examination announcement offers some clues to the subjects which will be tested. Think about the job itself. Review the duties in your mind. Can you perform them, or are there some in which you are rusty? Fill in the blank spots in your preparation.

Many jurisdictions preview the written test in the exam announcement by including a section called "Knowledge and Abilities Required," "Scope of the Examination," or some similar heading. Here you will find out specifically what fields will be tested.

2) Review your own background

Once you learn in general what the position is all about, and what you need to know to do the work, ask yourself which subjects you already know fairly well and which need improvement. You may wonder whether to concentrate on improving your strong areas or on building some background in your fields of weakness. When the announcement has specified "some knowledge" or "considerable knowledge," or has used adjectives like "beginning principles of..." or "advanced ... methods," you can get a clue as to the number and difficulty of questions to be asked in any given field. More questions, and hence broader coverage, would be included for those subjects which are more important in the work. Now weigh your strengths and weaknesses against the job requirements and prepare accordingly.

3) Determine the level of the position

Another way to tell how intensively you should prepare is to understand the level of the job for which you are applying. Is it the entering level? In other words, is this the position in which beginners in a field of work are hired? Or is it an intermediate or advanced level? Sometimes this is indicated by such words as "Junior" or "Senior" in the class title. Other jurisdictions use Roman numerals to designate the level – Clerk I, Clerk II, for example. The word "Supervisor" sometimes appears in the title. If the level is not indicated by the title, check the description of duties. Will you be working under very close supervision, or will you have responsibility for independent decisions in this work?

4) Choose appropriate study materials

Now that you know the subjects to be examined and the relative amount of each subject to be covered, you can choose suitable study materials. For beginning level jobs, or even advanced ones, if you have a pronounced weakness in some aspect of your training, read a modern, standard textbook in that field. Be sure it is up to date and has general coverage. Such books are normally available at your library, and the librarian will be glad to help you locate one. For entry-level positions, questions of appropriate difficulty are chosen – neither highly advanced questions, nor those too simple. Such questions require careful thought but not advanced training.

If the position for which you are applying is technical or advanced, you will read more advanced, specialized material. If you are already familiar with the basic principles of your field, elementary textbooks would waste your time. Concentrate on advanced textbooks and technical periodicals. Think through the concepts and review difficult problems in your field.

These are all general sources. You can get more ideas on your own initiative, following these leads. For example, training manuals and publications of the government agency which employs workers in your field can be useful, particularly for technical and professional positions. A letter or visit to the government department involved may result in more specific study suggestions, and certainly will provide you with a more definite idea of the exact nature of the position you are seeking.

III. KINDS OF TESTS

Tests are used for purposes other than measuring knowledge and ability to perform specified duties. For some positions, it is equally important to test ability to make adjustments to new situations or to profit from training. In others, basic mental abilities not dependent on information are essential. Questions which test these things may not appear as pertinent to the duties of the position as those which test for knowledge and information. Yet they are often highly important parts of a fair examination. For very general questions, it is almost impossible to help you direct your study efforts. What we can do is to point out some of the more common of these general abilities needed in public service positions and describe some typical questions.

1) General information

Broad, general information has been found useful for predicting job success in some kinds of work. This is tested in a variety of ways, from vocabulary lists to questions about current events. Basic background in some field of work, such as sociology or economics, may be sampled in a group of questions. Often these are principles which have become familiar to most persons through exposure rather than through formal training. It is difficult to advise you how to study for these questions; being alert to the world around you is our best suggestion.

2) Verbal ability

An example of an ability needed in many positions is verbal or language ability. Verbal ability is, in brief, the ability to use and understand words. Vocabulary and grammar tests are typical measures of this ability. Reading comprehension or paragraph interpretation questions are common in many kinds of civil service tests. You are given a paragraph of written material and asked to find its central meaning.

3) Numerical ability

Number skills can be tested by the familiar arithmetic problem, by checking paired lists of numbers to see which are alike and which are different, or by interpreting charts and graphs. In the latter test, a graph may be printed in the test booklet which you are asked to use as the basis for answering questions.

4) Observation

A popular test for law-enforcement positions is the observation test. A picture is shown to you for several minutes, then taken away. Questions about the picture test your ability to observe both details and larger elements.

5) Following directions

In many positions in the public service, the employee must be able to carry out written instructions dependably and accurately. You may be given a chart with several columns, each column listing a variety of information. The questions require you to carry out directions involving the information given in the chart.

6) Skills and aptitudes

Performance tests effectively measure some manual skills and aptitudes. When the skill is one in which you are trained, such as typing or shorthand, you can practice. These tests are often very much like those given in business school or high school courses. For many of the other skills and aptitudes, however, no short-time preparation can be made. Skills and abilities natural to you or that you have developed throughout your lifetime are being tested.

Many of the general questions just described provide all the data needed to answer the questions and ask you to use your reasoning ability to find the answers. Your best preparation for these tests, as well as for tests of facts and ideas, is to be at your physical and mental best. You, no doubt, have your own methods of getting into an exam-taking mood and keeping "in shape." The next section lists some ideas on this subject.

IV KINDS OF QUESTIONS

Only rarely is the "essay" question, which you answer in narrative form, used in civil service tests. Civil service tests are usually of the short-answer type. Full instructions for answering these questions will be given to you at the examination. But in case this is your first experience with short-answer questions and separate answer sheets, here is what you need to know:

1) Multiple-choice Questions

Most popular of the short-answer questions is the "multiple choice" or "best answer" question. It can be used, for example, to test for factual knowledge, ability to solve problems or judgment in meeting situations found at work.

A multiple-choice question is normally one of three types—

- It can begin with an incomplete statement followed by several possible endings. You are to find the one ending which *best* completes the statement, although some of the others may not be entirely wrong.
- It can also be a complete statement in the form of a question which is answered by choosing one of the statements listed.
- It can be in the form of a problem – again you select the best answer.

Here is an example of a multiple-choice question with a discussion which should give you some clues as to the method for choosing the right answer:

When an employee has a complaint about his assignment, the action which will *best* help him overcome his difficulty is to
A. discuss his difficulty with his coworkers
B. take the problem to the head of the organization
C. take the problem to the person who gave him the assignment
D. say nothing to anyone about his complaint

In answering this question, you should study each of the choices to find which is best. Consider choice "A" – Certainly an employee may discuss his complaint with fellow employees, but no change or improvement can result, and the complaint remains unresolved. Choice "B" is a poor choice since the head of the organization probably does not know what assignment you have been given, and taking your problem to him is known as "going over the head" of the supervisor. The supervisor, or person who made the assignment, is the person who can clarify it or correct any injustice. Choice "C" is, therefore, correct. To say nothing, as in choice "D," is unwise. Supervisors have and interest in knowing the problems employees are facing, and the employee is seeking a solution to his problem.

2) True/False Questions

The "true/false" or "right/wrong" form of question is sometimes used. Here a complete statement is given. Your job is to decide whether the statement is right or wrong.

SAMPLE: A person-to-person long-distance telephone call costs less than a station-to-station call to the same city.

This statement is wrong, or false, since person-to-person calls are more expensive.

This is not a complete list of all possible question forms, although most of the others are variations of these common types. You will always get complete directions for answering questions. Be sure you understand *how* to mark your answers – ask questions until you do.

V. RECORDING YOUR ANSWERS

For an examination with very few applicants, you may be told to record your answers in the test booklet itself. Separate answer sheets are much more common. If this separate answer sheet is to be scored by machine – and this is often the case – it is highly important that you mark your answers correctly in order to get credit.

An electric scoring machine is often used in civil service offices because of the speed with which papers can be scored. Machine-scored answer sheets must be marked with a pencil, which will be given to you. This pencil has a high graphite content which responds to the electric scoring machine. As a matter of fact, stray dots may register as answers, so do not let your pencil rest on the answer sheet while you are pondering the correct answer. Also, if your pencil lead breaks or is otherwise defective, ask for another.

Since the answer sheet will be dropped in a slot in the scoring machine, be careful not to bend the corners or get the paper crumpled.

The answer sheet normally has five vertical columns of numbers, with 30 numbers to a column. These numbers correspond to the question numbers in your test booklet. After each number, going across the page are four or five pairs of dotted lines. These short dotted lines have small letters or numbers above them. The first two pairs may also have a "T" or "F" above the letters. This indicates that the first two pairs only are to be used if the questions are of the true-false type. If the questions are multiple choice, disregard the "T" and "F" and pay attention only to the small letters or numbers.

Answer your questions in the manner of the sample that follows:

32. The largest city in the United States is
    A. Washington, D.C.
    B. New York City
    C. Chicago
    D. Detroit
    E. San Francisco

1) Choose the answer you think is best. (New York City is the largest, so "B" is correct.)
2) Find the row of dotted lines numbered the same as the question you are answering. (Find row number 32)
3) Find the pair of dotted lines corresponding to the answer. (Find the pair of lines under the mark "B.")
4) Make a solid black mark between the dotted lines.

VI. BEFORE THE TEST

Common sense will help you find procedures to follow to get ready for an examination. Too many of us, however, overlook these sensible measures. Indeed, nervousness and fatigue have been found to be the most serious reasons why applicants fail to do their best on civil service tests. Here is a list of reminders:

- Begin your preparation early – Don't wait until the last minute to go scurrying around for books and materials or to find out what the position is all about.
- Prepare continuously – An hour a night for a week is better than an all-night cram session. This has been definitely established. What is more, a night a

week for a month will return better dividends than crowding your study into a shorter period of time.

- Locate the place of the exam – You have been sent a notice telling you when and where to report for the examination. If the location is in a different town or otherwise unfamiliar to you, it would be well to inquire the best route and learn something about the building.
- Relax the night before the test – Allow your mind to rest. Do not study at all that night. Plan some mild recreation or diversion; then go to bed early and get a good night's sleep.
- Get up early enough to make a leisurely trip to the place for the test – This way unforeseen events, traffic snarls, unfamiliar buildings, etc. will not upset you.
- Dress comfortably – A written test is not a fashion show. You will be known by number and not by name, so wear something comfortable.
- Leave excess paraphernalia at home – Shopping bags and odd bundles will get in your way. You need bring only the items mentioned in the official notice you received; usually everything you need is provided. Do not bring reference books to the exam. They will only confuse those last minutes and be taken away from you when in the test room.
- Arrive somewhat ahead of time – If because of transportation schedules you must get there very early, bring a newspaper or magazine to take your mind off yourself while waiting.
- Locate the examination room – When you have found the proper room, you will be directed to the seat or part of the room where you will sit. Sometimes you are given a sheet of instructions to read while you are waiting. Do not fill out any forms until you are told to do so; just read them and be prepared.
- Relax and prepare to listen to the instructions
- If you have any physical problem that may keep you from doing your best, be sure to tell the test administrator. If you are sick or in poor health, you really cannot do your best on the exam. You can come back and take the test some other time.

VII. AT THE TEST

The day of the test is here and you have the test booklet in your hand. The temptation to get going is very strong. Caution! There is more to success than knowing the right answers. You must know how to identify your papers and understand variations in the type of short-answer question used in this particular examination. Follow these suggestions for maximum results from your efforts:

1) Cooperate with the monitor

The test administrator has a duty to create a situation in which you can be as much at ease as possible. He will give instructions, tell you when to begin, check to see that you are marking your answer sheet correctly, and so on. He is not there to guard you, although he will see that your competitors do not take unfair advantage. He wants to help you do your best.

2) Listen to all instructions

Don't jump the gun! Wait until you understand all directions. In most civil service tests you get more time than you need to answer the questions. So don't be in a hurry.

Read each word of instructions until you clearly understand the meaning. Study the examples, listen to all announcements and follow directions. Ask questions if you do not understand what to do.

3) Identify your papers

Civil service exams are usually identified by number only. You will be assigned a number; you must not put your name on your test papers. Be sure to copy your number correctly. Since more than one exam may be given, copy your exact examination title.

4) Plan your time

Unless you are told that a test is a "speed" or "rate of work" test, speed itself is usually not important. Time enough to answer all the questions will be provided, but this does not mean that you have all day. An overall time limit has been set. Divide the total time (in minutes) by the number of questions to determine the approximate time you have for each question.

5) Do not linger over difficult questions

If you come across a difficult question, mark it with a paper clip (useful to have along) and come back to it when you have been through the booklet. One caution if you do this – be sure to skip a number on your answer sheet as well. Check often to be sure that you have not lost your place and that you are marking in the row numbered the same as the question you are answering.

6) Read the questions

Be sure you know what the question asks! Many capable people are unsuccessful because they failed to *read* the questions correctly.

7) Answer all questions

Unless you have been instructed that a penalty will be deducted for incorrect answers, it is better to guess than to omit a question.

8) Speed tests

It is often better NOT to guess on speed tests. It has been found that on timed tests people are tempted to spend the last few seconds before time is called in marking answers at random – without even reading them – in the hope of picking up a few extra points. To discourage this practice, the instructions may warn you that your score will be "corrected" for guessing. That is, a penalty will be applied. The incorrect answers will be deducted from the correct ones, or some other penalty formula will be used.

9) Review your answers

If you finish before time is called, go back to the questions you guessed or omitted to give them further thought. Review other answers if you have time.

10) Return your test materials

If you are ready to leave before others have finished or time is called, take ALL your materials to the monitor and leave quietly. Never take any test material with you. The monitor can discover whose papers are not complete, and taking a test booklet may be grounds for disqualification.

VIII. EXAMINATION TECHNIQUES

1) Read the general instructions carefully. These are usually printed on the first page of the exam booklet. As a rule, these instructions refer to the timing of the examination; the fact that you should not start work until the signal and must stop work at a signal, etc. If there are any *special* instructions, such as a choice of questions to be answered, make sure that you note this instruction carefully.

2) When you are ready to start work on the examination, that is as soon as the signal has been given, read the instructions to each question booklet, underline any key words or phrases, such as *least, best, outline, describe* and the like. In this way you will tend to answer as requested rather than discover on reviewing your paper that you *listed without describing*, that you selected the *worst* choice rather than the *best* choice, etc.

3) If the examination is of the objective or multiple-choice type – that is, each question will also give a series of possible answers: A, B, C or D, and you are called upon to select the best answer and write the letter next to that answer on your answer paper – it is advisable to start answering each question in turn. There may be anywhere from 50 to 100 such questions in the three or four hours allotted and you can see how much time would be taken if you read through all the questions before beginning to answer any. Furthormore, if you come across a question or group of questions which you know would be difficult to answer, it would undoubtedly affect your handling of all the other questions.

4) If the examination is of the essay type and contains but a few questions, it is a moot point as to whether you should read all the questions before starting to answer any one. Of course, if you are given a choice – say five out of seven and the like – then it is essential to read all the questions so you can eliminate the two that are most difficult. If, however, you are asked to answer all the questions, there may be danger in trying to answer the easiest one first because you may find that you will spend too much time on it. The best technique is to answer the first question, then proceed to the second, etc.

5) Time your answers. Before the exam begins, write down the time it started, then add the time allowed for the examination and write down the time it must be completed, then divide the time available somewhat as follows:
   - If 3-1/2 hours are allowed, that would be 210 minutes. If you have 80 objective-type questions, that would be an average of 2-1/2 minutes per question. Allow yourself no more than 2 minutes per question, or a total of 160 minutes, which will permit about 50 minutes to review.
   - If for the time allotment of 210 minutes there are 7 essay questions to answer, that would average about 30 minutes a question. Give yourself only 25 minutes per question so that you have about 35 minutes to review.

6) The most important instruction is to *read each question* and make sure you know what is wanted. The second most important instruction is to *time yourself properly* so that you answer every question. The third most

important instruction is to *answer every question.* Guess if you have to but include something for each question. Remember that you will receive no credit for a blank and will probably receive some credit if you write something in answer to an essay question. If you guess a letter – say "B" for a multiple-choice question – you may have guessed right. If you leave a blank as an answer to a multiple-choice question, the examiners may respect your feelings but it will not add a point to your score. Some exams may penalize you for wrong answers, so in such cases *only,* you may not want to guess unless you have some basis for your answer.

7) Suggestions
   a. Objective-type questions
      1. Examine the question booklet for proper sequence of pages and questions
      2. Read all instructions carefully
      3. Skip any question which seems too difficult; return to it after all other questions have been answered
      4. Apportion your time properly; do not spend too much time on any single question or group of questions
      5. Note and underline key words – *all, most, fewest, least, best, worst, same, opposite,* etc.
      6. Pay particular attention to negatives
      7. Note unusual option, e.g., unduly long, short, complex, different or similar in content to the body of the question
      8. Observe the use of "hedging" words – *probably, may, most likely,* etc.
      9. Make sure that your answer is put next to the same number as the question
      10. Do not second-guess unless you have good reason to believe the second answer is definitely more correct
      11. Cross out original answer if you decide another answer is more accurate; do not erase until you are ready to hand your paper in
      12. Answer all questions; guess unless instructed otherwise
      13. Leave time for review

   b. Essay questions
      1. Read each question carefully
      2. Determine exactly what is wanted. Underline key words or phrases.
      3. Decide on outline or paragraph answer
      4. Include many different points and elements unless asked to develop any one or two points or elements
      5. Show impartiality by giving pros and cons unless directed to select one side only
      6. Make and write down any assumptions you find necessary to answer the questions
      7. Watch your English, grammar, punctuation and choice of words
      8. Time your answers; don't crowd material

8) Answering the essay question

Most essay questions can be answered by framing the specific response around several key words or ideas. Here are a few such key words or ideas:

M's: manpower, materials, methods, money, management
P's: purpose, program, policy, plan, procedure, practice, problems, pitfalls, personnel, public relations
  a. Six basic steps in handling problems:
     1. Preliminary plan and background development
     2. Collect information, data and facts
     3. Analyze and interpret information, data and facts
     4. Analyze and develop solutions as well as make recommendations
     5. Prepare report and sell recommendations
     6. Install recommendations and follow up effectiveness

  b. Pitfalls to avoid
     1. *Taking things for granted* – A statement of the situation does not necessarily imply that each of the elements is necessarily true; for example, a complaint may be invalid and biased so that all that can be taken for granted is that a complaint has been registered
     2. *Considering only one side of a situation* – Wherever possible, indicate several alternatives and then point out the reasons you selected the best one
     3. *Failing to indicate follow up* – Whenever your answer indicates action on your part, make certain that you will take proper follow-up action to see how successful your recommendations, procedures or actions turn out to be
     4. *Taking too long in answering any single question* – Remember to time your answers properly

IX. AFTER THE TEST

   Scoring procedures differ in detail among civil service jurisdictions although the general principles are the same. Whether the papers are hand-scored or graded by machine we have described, they are nearly always graded by number. That is, the person who marks the paper knows only the number – never the name – of the applicant. Not until all the papers have been graded will they be matched with names. If other tests, such as training and experience or oral interview ratings have been given, scores will be combined. Different parts of the examination usually have different weights. For example, the written test might count 60 percent of the final grade, and a rating of training and experience 40 percent. In many jurisdictions, veterans will have a certain number of points added to their grades.
   After the final grade has been determined, the names are placed in grade order and an eligible list is established. There are various methods for resolving ties between those who get the same final grade – probably the most common is to place first the name of the person whose application was received first. Job offers are made from the eligible list in the order the names appear on it. You will be notified of your grade and your rank as soon as all these computations have been made. This will be done as rapidly as possible.
   People who are found to meet the requirements in the announcement are called "eligibles." Their names are put on a list of eligible candidates. An eligible's chances of getting a job depend on how high he stands on this list and how fast agencies are filling jobs from the list.

When a job is to be filled from a list of eligibles, the agency asks for the names of people on the list of eligibles for that job. When the civil service commission receives this request, it sends to the agency the names of the three people highest on this list. Or, if the job to be filled has specialized requirements, the office sends the agency the names of the top three persons who meet these requirements from the general list.

The appointing officer makes a choice from among the three people whose names were sent to him. If the selected person accepts the appointment, the names of the others are put back on the list to be considered for future openings.

That is the rule in hiring from all kinds of eligible lists, whether they are for typist, carpenter, chemist, or something else. For every vacancy, the appointing officer has his choice of any one of the top three eligibles on the list. This explains why the person whose name is on top of the list sometimes does not get an appointment when some of the persons lower on the list do. If the appointing officer chooses the second or third eligible, the No. 1 eligible does not get a job at once, but stays on the list until he is appointed or the list is terminated.

X. HOW TO PASS THE INTERVIEW TEST

The examination for which you applied requires an oral interview test. You have already taken the written test and you are now being called for the interview test – the final part of the formal examination.

You may think that it is not possible to prepare for an interview test and that there are no procedures to follow during an interview. Our purpose is to point out some things you can do in advance that will help you and some good rules to follow and pitfalls to avoid while you are being interviewed.

What is an interview supposed to test?

The written examination is designed to test the technical knowledge and competence of the candidate; the oral is designed to evaluate intangible qualities, not readily measured otherwise, and to establish a list showing the relative fitness of each candidate – as measured against his competitors – for the position sought. Scoring is not on the basis of "right" and "wrong," but on a sliding scale of values ranging from "not passable" to "outstanding." As a matter of fact, it is possible to achieve a relatively low score without a single "incorrect" answer because of evident weakness in the qualities being measured.

Occasionally, an examination may consist entirely of an oral test – either an individual or a group oral. In such cases, information is sought concerning the technical knowledges and abilities of the candidate, since there has been no written examination for this purpose. More commonly, however, an oral test is used to supplement a written examination.

Who conducts interviews?

The composition of oral boards varies among different jurisdictions. In nearly all, a representative of the personnel department serves as chairman. One of the members of the board may be a representative of the department in which the candidate would work. In some cases, "outside experts" are used, and, frequently, a businessman or some other representative of the general public is asked to serve. Labor and management or other special groups may be represented. The aim is to secure the services of experts in the appropriate field.

However the board is composed, it is a good idea (and not at all improper or unethical) to ascertain in advance of the interview who the members are and what groups they represent. When you are introduced to them, you will have some idea of their backgrounds and interests, and at least you will not stutter and stammer over their names.

What should be done before the interview?

While knowledge about the board members is useful and takes some of the surprise element out of the interview, there is other preparation which is more substantive. It *is* possible to prepare for an oral interview – in several ways:

1) Keep a copy of your application and review it carefully before the interview

This may be the only document before the oral board, and the starting point of the interview. Know what education and experience you have listed there, and the sequence and dates of all of it. Sometimes the board will ask you to review the highlights of your experience for them; you should not have to hem and haw doing it.

2) Study the class specification and the examination announcement

Usually, the oral board has one or both of these to guide them. The qualities, characteristics or knowledges required by the position sought are stated in these documents. They offer valuable clues as to the nature of the oral interview. For example, if the job involves supervisory responsibilities, the announcement will usually indicate that knowledge of modern supervisory methods and the qualifications of the candidate as a supervisor will be tested. If so, you can expect such questions, frequently in the form of a hypothetical situation which you are expected to solve. NEVER go into an oral without knowledge of the duties and responsibilities of the job you seek.

3) Think through each qualification required

Try to visualize the kind of questions you would ask if you were a board member. How well could you answer them? Try especially to appraise your own knowledge and background in each area, *measured against the job sought*, and identify any areas in which you are weak. Be critical and realistic – do not flatter yourself.

4) Do some general reading in areas in which you feel you may be weak

For example, if the job involves supervision and your past experience has NOT, some general reading in supervisory methods and practices, particularly in the field of human relations, might be useful. Do NOT study agency procedures or detailed manuals. The oral board will be testing your understanding and capacity, not your memory.

5) Get a good night's sleep and watch your general health and mental attitude

You will want a clear head at the interview. Take care of a cold or any other minor ailment, and of course, no hangovers.

What should be done on the day of the interview?

Now comes the day of the interview itself. Give yourself plenty of time to get there. Plan to arrive somewhat ahead of the scheduled time, particularly if your appointment is in the fore part of the day. If a previous candidate fails to appear, the board might be ready for you a bit early. By early afternoon an oral board is almost invariably behind schedule if there are many candidates, and you may have to wait.

Take along a book or magazine to read, or your application to review, but leave any extraneous material in the waiting room when you go in for your interview. In any event, relax and compose yourself.

The matter of dress is important. The board is forming impressions about you – from your experience, your manners, your attitude, and your appearance. Give your personal appearance careful attention. Dress your best, but not your flashiest. Choose conservative, appropriate clothing, and be sure it is immaculate. This is a business interview, and your appearance should indicate that you regard it as such. Besides, being well groomed and properly dressed will help boost your confidence.

Sooner or later, someone will call your name and escort you into the interview room. *This is it.* From here on you are on your own. It is too late for any more preparation. But remember, you asked for this opportunity to prove your fitness, and you are here because your request was granted.

What happens when you go in?

The usual sequence of events will be as follows: The clerk (who is often the board stenographer) will introduce you to the chairman of the oral board, who will introduce you to the other members of the board. Acknowledge the introductions before you sit down. Do not be surprised if you find a microphone facing you or a stenotypist sitting by. Oral interviews are usually recorded in the event of an appeal or other review.

Usually the chairman of the board will open the interview by reviewing the highlights of your education and work experience from your application – primarily for the benefit of the other members of the board, as well as to get the material into the record. Do not interrupt or comment unless there is an error or significant misinterpretation; if that is the case, do not hesitate. But do not quibble about insignificant matters. Also, he will usually ask you some question about your education, experience or your present job – partly to get you to start talking and to establish the interviewing "rapport." He may start the actual questioning, or turn it over to one of the other members. Frequently, each member undertakes the questioning on a particular area, one in which he is perhaps most competent, so you can expect each member to participate in the examination. Because time is limited, you may also expect some rather abrupt switches in the direction the questioning takes, so do not be upset by it. Normally, a board member will not pursue a single line of questioning unless he discovers a particular strength or weakness.

After each member has participated, the chairman will usually ask whether any member has any further questions, then will ask you if you have anything you wish to add. Unless you are expecting this question, it may floor you. Worse, it may start you off on an extended, extemporaneous speech. The board is not usually seeking more information. The question is principally to offer you a last opportunity to present further qualifications or to indicate that you have nothing to add. So, if you feel that a significant qualification or characteristic has been overlooked, it is proper to point it out in a sentence or so. Do not compliment the board on the thoroughness of their examination – they have been sketchy, and you know it. If you wish, merely say, "No thank you, I have nothing further to add." This is a point where you can "talk yourself out" of a good impression or fail to present an important bit of information. Remember, *you close the interview yourself.*

The chairman will then say, "That is all, Mr. _____, thank you." Do not be startled; the interview is over, and quicker than you think. Thank him, gather your belongings and take your leave. Save your sigh of relief for the other side of the door.

How to put your best foot forward

Throughout this entire process, you may feel that the board individually and collectively is trying to pierce your defenses, seek out your hidden weaknesses and embarrass and confuse you. Actually, this is not true. They are obliged to make an appraisal of your qualifications for the job you are seeking, and they want to see you in your best light. Remember, they must interview all candidates and a non-cooperative candidate may become a failure in spite of their best efforts to bring out his qualifications. Here are 15 suggestions that will help you:

1) Be natural – Keep your attitude confident, not cocky

If you are not confident that you can do the job, do not expect the board to be. Do not apologize for your weaknesses, try to bring out your strong points. The board is interested in a positive, not negative, presentation. Cockiness will antagonize any board member and make him wonder if you are covering up a weakness by a false show of strength.

2) Get comfortable, but don't lounge or sprawl

Sit erectly but not stiffly. A careless posture may lead the board to conclude that you are careless in other things, or at least that you are not impressed by the importance of the occasion. Either conclusion is natural, even if incorrect. Do not fuss with your clothing, a pencil or an ashtray. Your hands may occasionally be useful to emphasize a point; do not let them become a point of distraction.

3) Do not wisecrack or make small talk

This is a serious situation, and your attitude should show that you consider it as such. Further, the time of the board is limited – they do not want to waste it, and neither should you.

4) Do not exaggerate your experience or abilities

In the first place, from information in the application or other interviews and sources, the board may know more about you than you think. Secondly, you probably will not get away with it. An experienced board is rather adept at spotting such a situation, so do not take the chance.

5) If you know a board member, do not make a point of it, yet do not hide it

Certainly you are not fooling him, and probably not the other members of the board. Do not try to take advantage of your acquaintanceship – it will probably do you little good.

6) Do not dominate the interview

Let the board do that. They will give you the clues – do not assume that you have to do all the talking. Realize that the board has a number of questions to ask you, and do not try to take up all the interview time by showing off your extensive knowledge of the answer to the first one.

7) Be attentive

You only have 20 minutes or so, and you should keep your attention at its sharpest throughout. When a member is addressing a problem or question to you, give him your undivided attention. Address your reply principally to him, but do not exclude the other board members.

8) Do not interrupt

A board member may be stating a problem for you to analyze. He will ask you a question when the time comes. Let him state the problem, and wait for the question.

9) Make sure you understand the question

Do not try to answer until you are sure what the question is. If it is not clear, restate it in your own words or ask the board member to clarify it for you. However, do not haggle about minor elements.

10) Reply promptly but not hastily

A common entry on oral board rating sheets is "candidate responded readily," or "candidate hesitated in replies." Respond as promptly and quickly as you can, but do not jump to a hasty, ill-considered answer.

11) Do not be peremptory in your answers

A brief answer is proper – but do not fire your answer back. That is a losing game from your point of view. The board member can probably ask questions much faster than you can answer them.

12) Do not try to create the answer you think the board member wants

He is interested in what kind of mind you have and how it works – not in playing games. Furthermore, he can usually spot this practice and will actually grade you down on it.

13) Do not switch sides in your reply merely to agree with a board member

Frequently, a member will take a contrary position merely to draw you out and to see if you are willing and able to defend your point of view. Do not start a debate, yet do not surrender a good position. If a position is worth taking, it is worth defending.

14) Do not be afraid to admit an error in judgment if you are shown to be wrong

The board knows that you are forced to reply without any opportunity for careful consideration. Your answer may be demonstrably wrong. If so, admit it and get on with the interview.

15) Do not dwell at length on your present job

The opening question may relate to your present assignment. Answer the question but do not go into an extended discussion. You are being examined for a *new* job, not your present one. As a matter of fact, try to phrase ALL your answers in terms of the job for which you are being examined.

Basis of Rating

Probably you will forget most of these "do's" and "don'ts" when you walk into the oral interview room. Even remembering them all will not ensure you a passing grade. Perhaps you did not have the qualifications in the first place. But remembering them will help you to put your best foot forward, without treading on the toes of the board members.

Rumor and popular opinion to the contrary notwithstanding, an oral board wants you to make the best appearance possible. They know you are under pressure – but they also want to see how you respond to it as a guide to what your reaction would be under the pressures of the job you seek. They will be influenced by the degree of poise you display, the personal traits you show and the manner in which you respond.

EXAMINATION SECTION

EXAMINATION SECTION
TEST 1

DIRECTIONS: Each question or incomplete statement is followed by several suggested answers or completions. Select the one that BEST answers the question or completes the statement. *PRINT THE LETTER OF THE CORRECT ANSWER IN TEE SPACE AT THE RIGHT.*

1. Police Communications Technicians must connect the caller to Transit Police when an incident occurs on a subway train or in the subway station.
    Which one of the following calls should be reported to Transit Police?

    A.   The newsstand outside the entrance to the 86th Street subway was just robbed, and the suspects fled down the street.
    B.   Soon after James Pike left the Columbus Circle subway station, his chain was snatched on the street corner.
    C.   While traveling to work on the *D* line subway train, John Smith was mugged.
    D.   A noisy group of school children have just come out of the Times Square subway station and are now annoying passersby on the street.

1.____

Question 2.

DIRECTIONS: Question 2 is to be answered SOLELY on the basis of the following information.
    When a Police Communications Technician is notified by patrol cars that they are in a vehicular pursuit, the dispatcher should obtain the following in the order given:
    I.   Location of pursuit
    II. Type of vehicle, color of vehicle, and direction of travel
    III. Nature of offense
    IV. License plate number and state
    V.   Number of occupant(s) in vehicle
    VI. Identity of the patrol car in pursuit

2. Police Communications Dispatcher Johnson is working the 26th Division when an unknown patrol car announces via car radio that he is in pursuit of a white 1986 Cadillac traveling north on Vanbrunt Street from Ainsley Place. Dispatcher Johnson then asks the pursuing patrol car, *What is the car wanted for?* The Officer replies, *The car is wanted for a hit and run.*
    What information should Dispatcher Johnson obtain NEXT?

    A.   The number of occupant(s) in the vehicle
    B.   Location of pursuit
    C.   License plate number and state
    D.   Identity of the patrol car in pursuit

2.____

Question 3.

DIRECTIONS: Question 3 is to be answered SOLELY on the basis of the following information.

Robbery - involves the unlawful taking of property from a person by force or attempted use of immediate force.

<u>Robbery in Progress</u> - crime is occurring at the time the call came into 911, 5 minutes in the past or when suspects are still in the area.

3. Which of the following situations would be considered a ROBBERY IN PROGRESS?   3.___

   A. Female calls 911 stating that she has just arrived home and found her apartment has been robbed.
   B. Male calls 911 stating that he just discovered that someone picked his pocket.
   C. Female calls 911 stating that she saw a man grab an elderly woman's purse.
   D. Child calls 911 stating that some man is beating up his mother and is trying to take her purse.

4. On June 20, 2007 at 6:30 P.M., Police Communications Technician White receives a call   4.___
   from an anonymous complainant stating the following facts:

Incident:	Male with a gun sitting in a blue car
Location of Incident:	In front of 185 Hall St.
Description of Suspect:	Male, Black, bald, approximately 25 years old, dressed in red

   Dispatcher White needs to be accurate and clear when transferring above information to the police dispatcher. Which one of the following expresses the above information MOST clearly and accurately?

   A. On June 20, 2007 at 6:30 P.M., a call was received stating that a bald man, dressed in red, was in front of 185 Hall St. A black male, approximately 25 years old, is sitting in a blue car holding a gun.
   B. A call was received on June 20, 2007. at 6:30 P.M. stating that a bald black male, approximately 25 years old, who is dressed in red, is armed with a gun sitting in a blue car in front of 185 Hall St.
   C. A call was received on June 20, 2007 at 6:30 P.M. Sitting in a blue car in front of 185 Hall St. is a Black male, approximately 25 years old. Dressed in red with a bald head, a man is armed with a gun.
   D. A call was received stating that in front of 185 Hall St., a bald male, approximately 25 years old, dressed in red, is sitting in a blue car. A Black male is armed with a gun at 6:30 P.M. on June 20, 2007.

5. Police Communications Technician Dozier receives a call from a female who has just wit-   5.___
   nessed the following:

Incident:	White female police officer being assaulted
Location of Incident:	Surf Avenue and West 30th Street, in front of a candy store
Description of Suspectp;	Hispanic female wearing a green dress, possibly armed with a gun

   Dispatcher Dozier is about to relay the information to the dispatcher.
   Which one of the following expresses the above information MOST clearly and accurately?

   A. A call was received from a female on Surf Avenue and West 30th Street stating that a white female police officer is being assaulted by a Hispanic female wearing a green dress. She is possibly armed with a gun in front of a candy store.
   B. In front of a candy store at Surf Avenue and West 30th Street, a call was received from a female stating that a white female police officer is being assaulted by a Hispanic female wearing a green dress. She is possibly armed with a gun.

C. A call was received from a female stating that at the corner of Surf Avenue and West 30th Street in front of a candy store, there is a white female police officer being assaulted. The suspect is a Hispanic female wearing a green dress, who is possibly armed with a gun.

D. A call was received from a female stating that at the corner of West 30th Street and Surf Avenue, there is a white female police officer in front of a candy store being assaulted. She is wearing a green dress. The Hispanic female is possibly armed with a gun.

Questions 6-8.

DIRECTIONS: Questions 6 through 8 are to be answered SOLELY on the basis of the following passage.

At 10:35 A.M., Police Communications Technician Ross receives a second call from Mrs. Smith who is very upset because she has been waiting for the police and an ambulance since her first call, one hour ago. Mrs. Smith was mugged, and in resisting the attack, her nose was broken. The location of the incident is the uptown side of the subway station for the IND #2 train located at Jay Street and Borough Hall. Operator Ross advises Mrs. Smith to hold on and that she will check the status of her complaint. Operator Ross calls the Emergency Medical Service (EMS) and connects Mrs. Smith to the EMS operator. The EMS operator informs Mrs. Smith that an ambulance is coming from a far distance away and will be at the location at approximately 11:03 A.M. Operator Ross then calls the Transit Authority Police Department (TAPD). The TAPD received Mrs. Smith's first call at 9:37 A.M., and police arrived at location at 9:46 M. However, the police arrived at the downtown side of the subway station for the IND #3 train. TAPD informs Operator Ross that a police car will arrive at the correct location as soon as possible.

6. What is the CLOSEST approximate time that Mrs. Smith made her first call for help? _____ A.M.   6.____

A. 9:35   B. 9:46   C. 10:35   D. 11:03 .

7. The ambulance was delayed because   7.____

A. the ambulance responded to the downtown side of the subway station for the IND #2 train
B. EMS never received Mrs. Smith's request for an ambulance
C. a broken nose is not a priority request for an ambulance
D. the ambulance was coming from a far distance

8. There was a delay in TAPD response to the crime scene because TAPD   8.____

A. was coming from a far distance
B. responded on the uptown side of the subway station for the IND #2 train
C. was waiting for the -Police Department to respond first
D. responded on the downtown side of the subway station for the IND #3 train

9. Extreme care must be taken when assigning solo cars (one police officer in a vehicle) to   9.___
incidents. If anything in the job indicates that the job may be a potentially violent situation, a solo car should not be assigned.
In which one of the following incidents should a Police Communications Technician
assign a solo car?
A

   A. disorderly male carrying a knife
   B. house that was broken into two days ago
   C. suspiciously occupied auto
   D. group of rowdy teenagers throwing beer bottles at passersbys

Question 10.

DIRECTIONS: Question 10 is to be answered SOLELY on the basis of the following informa-
              tion.
On the Police Communications Technician's screen, the following incidents appear which
were called in at the same time:
     I. Caller states that she is looking out her 10th floor window and sees a man
        sleeping on the street in front of her home at Crescent Street and 4th Avenue.
    II. Caller states that he was driving down the block of Crescent Street between
        3rd and 4th Avenues and just witnessed a man being beaten and mugged. The
        caller thinks that the victim is unconscious.
   III. Caller states there is a car accident at Crescent Street and 3rd Avenue, and
        one of the passengers suffered a broken arm.

10. Which of the above should the operator MOST likely consider as the same incident?   10.___

   A. I and II   B. II and III
   C. I and III   D. I, II, and III

11. Police Communications Operator Raymond receives a call regarding a rape and obtains   11.___
the following information:
Time of Rape: 10:35 P.M.
Place of Rape: Sam's Laundromat, 200 Melrose Avenue
Victim: Joan McGraw
Crime: Rape
Suspect: Male, Hispanic, carrying a gun
Operator Raymond is about to enter the incident into the computer.
Which one of the following expresses the above information MOST clearly and accu-
rately?

   A. At 10:35 P.M., Joan McGraw was raped in Sam's Laundromat, located at 200 Mel-
      rose Avenue, by a Hispanic male carrying a gun.
   B. A Hispanic male was carrying a gun at 10:35 P.M. Joan McGraw was raped in
      Sam's Laundromat located at 200 Melrose Avenue.
   C. Carrying a gun, Joan McGraw was raped by a Hispanic male. This occurred in
      Sam's Laundromat located at 200 Melrose Avenue at 10:35 P.M.
   D. At 10:35 P.M., Joan McGraw was raped by a Hispanic male carrying a gun. Sam's
      Laundromat is located at 200 Melrose Avenue.

12. Police Communications Dispatcher Gold receives a call concerning a disorderly male in   12.____
a local drug store. He obtains the following information:

Place of Occurrence: Rapid-Serve Drug Store
Complainant: George Meyer
Crime: Threatening gestures and abusive language
Suspect: Male, white
Action Taken: The suspect was removed from premises by the police.

Dispatcher Gold is about to enter the incident into the computer.
Which one of the following expresses the above information MOST clearly and accurately?

   A.   George Meyer called the police because a white male was removed from the Rapid-Serve Drug Store. He was making threatening gestures and using abusive language.

   B.   George Meyer called the police and was removed from the Rapid-Serve Drug Store. A white male was making threatening gestures and using abusive language.

   C.   At the Rapid-Serve Drug Store, a white male was making threatening gestures and using abusive language. George Meyer called the police and removed the suspect from the drug store.

   D.   George Meyer called the police because a white male was making threatening gestures and using abusive language in the Rapid-Serve Drug Store. The suspect was removed from the drug store by the police.

Question 13.

DIRECTIONS: Question 13 is to be answered SOLELY on the basis of the following information.

When dispatching an incident involving a suspicious package, a Police Communications Technician should do the following in the order given:

   I.   Assign a patrol car and Patrol Sergeant.
   II.   Enter into the computer additional information received from assigned cars.
   III.   Notify appropriate Emergency Assistance.
   IV.   Notify the Bomb Squad.
   V.   Notify the Duty Captain.

13. Police Communications Technician Berlin receives a call involving a suspicious package   13.____
located on the corner of Gates Avenue and Blake Street. Dispatcher Berlin promptly assigns a patrol car and a Patrol Sergeant to the incident. Upon arrival, the Sergeant determines that there is a ticking sound coming from the box. The Sergeant immediately advises Dispatcher Berlin of the situation and tells Dispatcher Berlin to call the Fire Department and have them respond.
What should Dispatcher Berlin to NEXT?

   A.   Call the Fire Department.
   B.   Notify the Bomb Squad.
   C.   Enter additional information received from assigned cars into the computer.
   D.   Notify the Duty Captain.

Questions 14-16.

DIRECTIONS: Questions 14 through 16 are to be answered SOLELY on the basis of the following passage.

Police Communications Technician Robbins receives a call at 5:15 P.M. from Mr. Adams reporting he witnessed a shooting in front of 230 Eagle Road. Mr. Adams, who lives at 234 Eagle Road, states he overheard two white males arguing with a Black man. He describes one white male as having blonde hair and wearing a black jacket with blue jeans, and the other white male as having brown hair and wearing a white jacket and blue jeans.

Mr. Adams recognized the Black man as John Rivers, the son of Mrs. Mary Rivers, who lives at 232 Eagle Road. At 5:10 P.M., the blonde male took a gun, shot John in the stomach, and dragged his body into the alleyway. The two males ran into the backyard of 240 Eagle Road and headed west on Randall Boulevard. Dispatcher Robbins connects Mr. Adams to the Emergency Medical Service. The Ambulance Receiving Operator processes the call at 5:25 P.M. and advises Mr. Adams that the next available ambulance will be sent.

14. Who was the eyewitness to the shooting?   14.___

    A. Dispatcher Robbins   B. Mr. Adams
    C. Mrs. Rivers   D. John Rivers

15. In front of what address was John Rivers shot?   15.___
    _____ Eagle Road.

    A. 230   B. 232   C. 234   D. 240

16. What is the description of the male who fired the gun? A male wearing a _____ jacket   16.___
and blue jeans.

    A. white blonde-haired; white
    B. white brown-haired; black
    C. white blonde-haired; black
    D. Black brown-haired; white

17. A Police Communications Technician can have several calls for police response on their   17.___
computer screen at one time. A dispatcher may have to determine which of the calls is the most serious and assign that one to the police first.
Which one of the following situations should a dispatcher assign to the police FIRST?

    A. A robbery which occurred two hours ago, and the suspects have fled the scene
    B. A suspicious man offering a child candy to get the child into his van at the time of the call
    C. A woman returns to her car and finds her left fender dented
    D. A group of youths playing cards in the hallway

18. The following information was obtained by Police Communications Technician Fried   18.___
regarding a call of an auto accident with injuries:
Date of Accident: March 7, 2007
Place of Accident: 50 West 96th Street
Time of Accident: 3:15 P.M.
Drivers: Susan Green and Nancy White

Injured: Nancy White

Action Taken: Emergency Medical Services (EMS) Operator 600 was notified

Dispatcher Fried is about to enter the above information into the computer.

Which one of the following expresses the above information MOST clearly and accurately?

A. At 50 West 96th Street, Susan Green and Nancy White had an auto accident resulting in an injury to Nancy White. EMS Operator 600 was notifed to send an ambulance at 3:15 P.M. on March 7, 2007.

B. EMS Operator 600 was notified to send an ambulance to 50 West 96th Street due to an auto accident between Nancy White and Susan Green, who was injured on March 7, 2007 at 3:15 P.M.

C. Susan Green and Nancy White were involved in an auto accident at 50 West 96th Street on March 7, 2007. At 3:15 P.M., EMS Operator 600 was notified to send an ambulance for Nancy White.

D. On March 7, 2007 at 3:15 P.M., Susan Green and Nancy White were involved in an auto accident at 50 West 96th Street. EMS Operator 600 was notified to send an ambulance for Nancy White who was injured in the accident.

Questions 19-20.

DIRECTIONS: Questions 19 and 20 are to be answered SOLELY on the basis of the following information.

At the beginning of their tours, Police Communications Technicians need to call the precinct to find out what patrol cars are covering which sections of the precinct and which special assignment cars are being used. Special assignment cars are used instead of regular patrol cars when certain situations arise. Special assignment cars should be assigned before a patrol car when a call comes in that is related to the car's special assignment, regardless of what section the incident is occurring in. Otherwise, a regular patrol car should be assigned.

Police Communications Technician Tanner is assigned to the 83rd Precinct. He calls the precinct and determines the following patrol cars and special assignment cars are being used:

Patrol cars are assigned as follows:
    Patrol Car 83A - Covers Sections A, B, C
    Patrol Car 83D - Covers Sections D, E, F
    Patrol Car 83G - Covers Sections G, H, I

Special assignment cars are assigned as follows:
    83SP1 - Burglary Car
    83SP2 - Religious Establishment
    83SP8 - Anti-Crime (plainclothes officers)

19. Dispatcher Tanner receives a call located in the 83rd Precinct in *E* Section. Which car should be assigned?

19.____

    A. 83D   B. 83A   C. 83SP8   D. 83SP2

20. Dispatcher Tanner receives a call concerning a burglary in *B* Section. Which is the CORRECT car to be assigned?

20.____

    A. 83A   B. 83G   C. 83SP1   D. 83SP2

KEY (CORRECT ANSWERS)

1.	C	11.	A
2.	C	12.	D
3.	D	13.	C
4.	B	14.	B
5.	C	15.	A
6.	A	16.	C
7.	D	17.	B
8.	D	18.	D
9.	B	19.	A
10.	A	20.	C

TEST 2

DIRECTIONS: Each question or incomplete statement is followed by several suggested answers or completions. Select the one that BEST answers the question or completes the statement. *PRINT THE LETTER OF THE CORRECT ANSWER IN THE SPACE AT THE RIGHT.*

1. Police Communications Technician Daniel receives a call stating the following: 1.____
   Date and Time of Call: June 21, 2007 at 12:30 P.M.
   Incident: Shots being fired
   Location: The roof of a building, located between Moore Street and Bushwick Avenue, exact address unknown
   Suspect: Male
   Complainant: Mr. Bernard
   Comments: Mr. Bernard will be wearing a brown coat and will direct officers to location of the incident.
   Dispatcher Daniel is about to enter the information into the computer.
   Which one of the following expresses the above information MOST clearly and accurately?
   On June 21, 2007,

   A. at 12:30 P.M., Dispatcher Daniel receives a call from a complainant stating that a male is on a roof of a building with an unknown address firing a gun, and he is wearing a brown coat. The complainant, Mr. Bernard, will be in front of the building to direct the police to the exact location of the incident.
   B. a male is firing a gun from a roof, stated complainant Mr. Bernard to Dispatcher Daniel. This is at Moore Street and Bushwick Avenue. At 12:30 P.M., the caller will be at the location to direct the police to the building where the male is firing the gun. He is wearing a brown coat.
   C. at 12:30 P.M., Dispatcher Daniel receives a call from a complainant, Mr. Bernard, who states that at a building with an unknown address, located between Moore Street and Bushwick Avenue, a male is firing a gun from a roof. Mr. Bernard will be at the location wearing a brown coat to direct the police to the exact building.
   D. Dispatcher Daniel receives a call from a complainant, Mr. Bernard, who is calling from a building with an unknown address. He informs Dispatcher Daniel that a male is firing a gun from a roof of a building between Moore Street and Bushwick Avenue. At 12:30 P.M., Mr. Bernard will be wearing a brown coat to direct the police to the incident.

Questions 2-4.

DIRECTIONS: Questions 2 through 4 are to be answered SOLELY on the basis of the following passage.

Mrs. Arroyo returns from work one evening to find her door open and loud noise coming from her apartment. She peeks through the crack of the door and sees a white male moving rapidly through her apartment wearing blue jeans and a pink T-shirt. She runs to the nearest public telephone and dials 911. Police Communications Technician Ms. Lopez takes the call. Mrs. Arroyo informs Operator Lopez that there is a strange man in her apartment. The operator asks the caller for her address, apartment number, name, and telephone number, and then puts Mrs. Arroyo on hold. Operator Lopez enters the address in the computer and, realizing it is a high priority call, tries to notify the Radio Dispatcher directly by depressing the *hotline* button.

The Radio Dispatcher does not respond, and Operator Lopez realizes the *hotline* button is not working. The operator then continues to enter the rest of the information into the computer and notifies the caller that the police will respond. Operator Lopez then walks into the dispatcher's room to make sure the dispatcher received the information entered into the computer, and then notifies the supervisor of her malfunctioning equipment.

2. The operator notified her supervisor because 2.___

    A. the suspect was still in the apartment
    B. the *hotline* button was not working
    C. she could not enter the address in the computer
    D. it was a high priority call

3. What was the FIRST action the operator took after putting the complainant on hold? 3.___

    A. Entered the caller's telephone number and name in the computer.
    B. Walked into the dispatcher's room.
    C. Entered the caller's address into the computer.
    D. Tried to notify the Radio Dispatcher by depressing the *hotline* button.

4. Operator Lopez depressed the *hotline* button 4.___

    A. to check if the *hotline* button was working properly
    B. because it was a high priority call
    C. to make sure the dispatcher received the information entered into the computer
    D. because the computer was not working properly

Question 5.

DIRECTIONS: Question 5 is to be answered SOLELY on the basis of the following information.

    A Police Communications Technician occasionally receives calls from persons making threats against public officials, visiting dignitaries, or members of the Police Department. When this occurs, the Dispatcher should do the following in the order given:
        I. Obtain details of the threat
            (A) Who is being threatened and how
            (B) When it is going to happen
        II. Attempt to determine the sex and ethnicity of the caller
        III. Try to obtain the identity, address, and telephone number of the caller
        IV. Notify the supervisor

5. Police Communications Operator Frye receives a call and obtains from the caller that he 5.___
is going to shoot the mayor on Election Day. Operator Frye determine the caller to be a male with a heavy Hispanic accent. Operator Frye asks the male for his name, address, and phone number. The caller does not respond and hangs up.
What should Operator Frye do NEXT?

    A. Obtain details of the threats.
    B. Determine the sex and ethnicity of the caller.
    C. Obtain the identity, address, and phone number of the caller.
    D. Notify the supervisor.

Question 6.

DIRECTIONS: Question 6 is to be answered SOLELY on the basis of the following information.

A Police Communications Technician will call back complainants only under the following conditions:

1.   Dispatcher needs clarification of information previously received from the complainant and/or
2.   To notify the complainant that police need to gain entry to the location of the incident.

6.   In which one of the following situations should a Police Communications Technician call back the complainant?

   A.   While responding to an assigned incident, Patrol Car 79A gets a flat tire. Patrol Car 79A radios the dispatcher and advises the dispatcher to call the complainant and notify the complainant that there will be a delay in police response.
   B.   Patrol Car 83B is assigned to an incident that occurred approximately 30 minutes ago. Patrol Car 83B advises the dispatcher that he is coming from a far distance and the dispatcher should call the complainant to find out which is the best way to get to the incident location.
   C.   . Patrol Car 66B is on the scene of an incident and is having a problem gaining entry into the building. Patrol Car 66B asks the dispatcher to call the complainant and ask him to meet the police officers from the patrol car outside the building.
   D.   Patrol Car 90B is assigned to a burglary that occurred in the complainant's private home. It is raining heavily outside, so Patrol Car 90B asks the dispatcher to call and request the complainant to meet the police by the patrol car.

6._____

7.   Police Communications Dispatcher Blake receives a call reporting a bank robbery and obtains the following information:
Time of Robbery: 11:30 A.M.
Place of. Robbery: Fidelity Bank
Crime: Bank Robbery
Suspect: Male, white, wearing blue jeans, blue jacket, carrying a brown bag
Witness: Susan Lane of 731 Madison Avenue
Dispatcher Blake is about to inform his supervisor of the facts concerning the bank robbery.
Which one of the following expresses the above information MOST clearly and accurately?

   A.   At 11:30 A.M., the Fidelity Bank was robbed. Susan Lane lives at 731 Madison Avenue. The witness saw a white male wearing blue jeans, a blue jacket, and carrying a brown bag.
   B.   Susan Lane of 731 Madison Avenue witnessed the robbery of Fidelity Bank at 11:30 A.M. The suspect is a white male and was wearing blue jeans, a blue jacket, and carrying a brown bag.
   C.   Wearing blue jeans, a blue jacket, and carrying a brown bag, Susan Lane of 731 Madison Avenue saw a white male robbing the Fidelity Bank. The robbery was witnessed at 11:30 A.M.

7._____

D. At 11:30 A.M., Susan Lane of 731 Madison Avenue witnessed the robbery of the Fidelity Bank. A white male wore blue jeans, a blue jacket, and carried a brown bag.

8. Police Communications Technician Levine receives an incident for dispatch containing the following information:

Incident:	A female being beaten
Location:	In front of 385 Wall Street
Victim:	White female
Suspect:	White, male, wearing a grey shirt, possibly concealing a gun underneath his shirt

Dispatcher Levine is about to relay this information to the patrol car.
Which one of the following expresses the above information MOST clearly and accurately?

   A. A white female is being beaten by a white male wearing a grey shirt, who is possibly concealing a gun underneath his shirt. This is occurring in front of 385 Wall Street.
   B. A white male is beating a white female wearing a grey shirt. He is possibly concealing a gun underneath his shirt in front of 385 Wall Street.
   C. A female is being beaten in front of 385 Wall Street. A white male is possibly concealing a gun underneath his shirt. She is white, and the suspect is wearing a grey shirt.
   D. In front of 385 Wall Street, a white female is being beaten by a suspect, possibly concealing a gun underneath his shirt. A white male is wearing a grey shirt.

8.___

Questions 9-11.

DIRECTIONS: Questions 9 through 11 are to be answered SOLELY on the basis of the following passage.

Police Communications Technician John Clove receives a call from a Social Worker, Mrs. Norma Harris of Presbyterian Hospital, who states there is a 16-year-old teenager on the other line, speaking to Dr. Samuel Johnson, a psychologist at the hospital. The teenager is threatening suicide and claims that she is an out-patient, but refuses to give her name, address, or telephone number. She further states that the teenager took 100 pills of valium and is experiencing dizziness, numbness of the lips, and heart palpitations. The teenager tells Dr. Johnson that she wants to die because her boyfriend left her because she is pregnant.

Dr. Johnson is keeping her on the line persuading her to give her name, telephone number, and address. The Social Worker asks the dispatcher to trace the call. The dispatcher puts the caller on hold and informs his supervisor, Mrs. Ross, of the incident. The supervisor contacts Telephone Technician Mr. Ralph Taylor. Mr. Taylor contacts the telephone company and speaks to Supervisor Wallace, asking him to trace the call between Dr. Johnson and the teenager. After approximately 10 minutes, the dispatcher gets back to the Social Worker and informs her that the call is being traced.

9. Why did the Social Worker call Dispatcher Clove?

   A. A teenager is threatening suicide.
   B. Mrs. Ross took 100 pills of valium.

9.___

C. Dr. Johnson felt dizzy, numbness of the lips, and heart palpitations.
D. An unmarried teenager is pregnant.

10. Who did Mr. Clove notify FIRST?   10._____

    A. Mrs. Norma Harris   B. Dr. Samuel Johnson
    C. Mr. Wallace   D. Mrs. Ross

11. The conversation between which two individuals is being traced?   11._____

    A. Mrs. Norma Harris and the 16-year-old teenager
    B. The Telephone Technician and Telephone Company Supervisor
    C. Dr. Johnson and the 16-year-old teenager
    D. The dispatcher and the Hospital Social Worker

Question 12.

DIRECTIONS: Question 12 is to be answered SOLELY on the basis of the following information.

On the Police Communications Technician's screen, the following incidents appear which were called in at the same time by three different callers:

    I.   A fight is occurring at 265 Hall Street between Myrtle and Willoughby Ave. The fight started in Apartment 3C, and the two men are now fighting in the street.
    II.   A fight took place between a security guard and a suspected shoplifter in a store at Hall St. and Willoughby Ave. The security guard is holding the suspect in the security office.
    III.   A fight is occurring between two white males on the street near the corner of Hall Street and Myrtle Ave. One of the males has a baseball bat.

12. Which of the above should a Police Communications Technician MOST likely consider as the same incident?   12._____

    A. I and II   B. II and III
    C. I and III   D. I, II, and III

Questions 13-15.

DIRECTIONS: Questions 13 through 15 are to be answered SOLELY on the basis of the following passage.

Police Communications Technician Flood receives a call from Mr. Michael Watkins, Program Director for *Meals on Wheels,* a program that delivers food to elderly people who cannot leave their home. Mr. Watkins states he received a call from Rochelle Berger, whose elderly aunt, Estelle Sims, is a client of his. Rochelle Berger informed Mr. Watkins that she has just received a call from her aunt's neighbor, Sally Bowles, who told her that her aunt has not eaten in several days and is in need of medical attention.

After questioning Mr. Watkins, Dispatcher Flood is informed that Estelle Sims lives at 300 79th Street in Apartment 6K, and her telephone number is 686-4527; Sally Bowles lives in Apartment 6H, and her telephone number is 678-2456. Mr. Watkins further advises that if there is difficulty getting into Estelle Sims' apartment, to ring Sally Bowies' bell and she will let you in. Mr. Watkins gives his phone number as 776-0451, and Rochelle Berger's phone number is 291-7287. Dispatcher Flood advises Mr. Watkins that the appropriate medical assistance will be sent.

13. Who did Sally Bowles notify that her neighbor needed medical attention?   13.__

    A. Dispatcher Flood   B. Michael Watkins
    C. Rochelle Berger   D. Estelle Sims

14. If the responding medical personnel are unable to get into Apartment 6K, they should   14.__
    speak to

    A. Rochelle Berger   B. Sally Bowles
    C. Dispatcher Flood   D. Michael Watkins

15. Whose telephone number is 686-4527?   15.__

    A. Michael Watkins   B. Estelle Sims
    C. Sally Bowles   D. Rochelle Berger

16. Police Communications Technicians often receive calls regarding incidents where a   16.__
    response from the Fire Department may be necessary.
    In which one of the following situations would a request from the dispatcher for the Fire
    Department to respond be MOST critical?
    A(n)

    A. fire hydrant has been opened by children on a hot August afternoon
    B. abandoned auto is parked in front of a fire hydrant
    C. neighbor's cat has climbed up a tree and is stuck
    D. excited woman smells smoke coming from the floor below

Question 17.

DIRECTIONS: Question 17 is to be answered SOLELY on the basis of the following informa-
                  tion.
    When a patrol car confirms that a murder has taken place, the Police Communications
Technician should notify the following people in the order given:
        I. Patrol Sergeant
       II. Dispatching Supervisor
      III. Operations Unit
      IV. Crime Scene Unit
       V. Precinct Detective Unit
      VI. Duty Captain

17. Police Communications Technician Rodger assigns a patrol car to investigate a man who   17.__
    was shot and killed. The patrol car arrives on the scene and confirms that a murder has
    taken place. The Patrol Sergeant hears what has happened on his police radio and
    informs Dispatcher Rodger that he is going to respond to the scene. The Dispatching
    Supervisor walks over to Dispatcher Rodger and is informed of the situation.
    Who should Dispatcher Rodger notify NEXT?

    A. Operations Unit   B. Patrol Sergeant
    C. Precinct Detective Unit   D. Crime Scene Unit

18. Police Communications Technician Peterson receives a call from a woman inside the subway station reporting that her purse has just been snatched. Dispatcher Peterson obtained the following information relating to the crime:

Place of Occurrence: E. 42nd Street and Times Square
Time of Occurrence: 5:00 P.M.
Crime: Purse Snatched
Victim: Thelma Johnson
Description of Suspect: Black, female, brown hair, blue jeans, red T-shirt
Dispatcher Peterson is about to relay the information to the Transit Authority Police Dispatcher.
Which one of the following expresses the above information MOST clearly and accurately?

    A.   At 5:00 P.M., a brown-haired Black woman snatched a purse inside the subway station at E. 42nd Street and Times Square belonging to Thelma Johnson. She was wearing blue jeans and a red T-shirt.

    B.   A purse was snatched from Thelma Johnson by a woman with brown hair in the subway station at 5:00 P.M. A Black female was wearing blue jeans and a red T-shirt at E. 42nd Street and Times Square.

    C.   At 5:00 P.M., Thelma Johnson's purse was snatched inside the subway station at E. 42nd Street and Times Square. The suspect is a Black female with brown hair who is wearing blue jeans and a red T-shirt.

    D.   Thelma Johnson reported at 5:00 P.M. her purse was snatched. In the subway station at E. 42nd Street and Times Square, a Black female with brown hair was wearing blue jeans and a red T-shirt.

18.____

19. Police Communications Technician Hopkins receives a call of an assault and obtains the following information concerning the incident:

Place of Occurrence: Times Square
Time of Occurrence: 3:15 A.M.
Victim: Peter Polk
Victim's Address: 50 E. 60 Street
Suspect: Male, Hispanic, 5'6", 140 lbs., dressed in black
Injury: Broken nose
Action Taken: Victim transported to St. Luke's Hospital
Dispatcher Hopkins is about to enter the job into the computer system.
Which one of the following expresses the above information MOST clearly and accurately?

    A.   At 3:15 A.M., Peter Polk was assaulted in Times Square by a Hispanic male, 5'6", 140 lbs., dressed in black, suffering a broken nose. Mr. Polk lives at 50 E. 69 Street and was transported to St. Luke's Hospital.

    B.   At 3:15 A.M., Peter Polk was assaulted in Times Square by a Hispanic male, 5'6", 140 lbs., dressed in black, who lives at 50 E. 69 Street. Mr. Polk suffered a broken nose and was transported to St. Luke's Hospital.

    C.   Peter Polk, who lives at 50 E. 69 Street, was assaulted at 3:15 A.M. in Times Square by a Hispanic male, 5'6", 140 lbs., dressed in black. Mr. Polk suffered a broken nose and was transported to St. Luke's Hospital.

    D.   Living at 50 E. 69 Street, Mr. Polk suffered a broken nose and was transported to St. Luke's Hospital. At 3:15 A.M., Mr. Polk was assaulted by a Hispanic male, 5'6", 140 lbs., who was dressed in black.

19.____

20. A Police Communications Technician is required to determine which situations called in to 911 require police assistance and which calls require non-emergency assistance. Which one of the following calls should a dispatcher MOST likely refer to non-emergency assistance?   20.___

    A. Mr. Moss threatens the owner of Deluxe Deli with bodily harm for giving him incorrect change of twenty dollars.

    B. The manager refuses to take back Mrs. Thompson's defective toaster because she doesn't have a receipt. Mrs. Thompson leaves the store.

    C. Mrs. Frank is having a violent argument with the manager of Donna's Dress Shop because he is refusing to exchange a dress she recently purchased.

    D. The manager of Metro Supermarket refuses to take back a stale loaf of bread, so the consumer punches him in the face.

KEY (CORRECT ANSWERS)

1.	C		11.	C
2.	B		12.	C
3.	C		13.	C
4.	B		14.	B
5.	D		15.	B
6.	C		16.	D
7.	B		17.	A
8.	A		18.	C
9.	A		19.	C
10.	D		20.	B

EXAMINATION SECTION
TEST 1

DIRECTIONS: Each question or incomplete statement is followed by several suggested answers or completions. Select the one that BEST answers the question or completes the statement. *PRINT THE LETTER OF THE CORRECT ANSWER IN THE SPACE AT THE RIGHT.*

Questions 1-3.

DIRECTIONS: Questions 1 through 3 are to be answered SOLELY on the basis of the following passage.

On May 15 at 10:15 A.M., Mr. Price was returning to his home at 220 Kings Walk when he discovered two of his neighbor's apartment doors slightly opened. One neighbor, Mrs. Kagan, who lives alone in Apartment 1C, was away on vacation. The other apartment, IB, is occupied by Martin and Ruth Stone, an elderly couple, who usually take a walk everyday at 10:00 A.M. Fearing a robbery might be taking place, Mr. Price runs downstairs to Mr. White in Apartment BI to call the police. Police Communications Technician Johnson received the call at 10:20 A.M. Mr. Price gave his address and stated that two apartments were possibly being burglarized. Communications Technician Johnson verified the address in the computer and then asked Mr. Price for descriptions of the suspects. He explained that he had not seen anyone, but he believed that they were still inside the building. Communications Technician Johnson immediately notified the dispatcher who assigned two patrol cars at 10:25 A.M., while Mr. Price was still on the phone. Communications Technician Johnson told Mr. Price that the police were responding to the location.

1. Who called Communications Technician Johnson? 1.____

    A. Mrs. Kagan   B. Mr. White
    C. Mrs. Stone   D. Mr. Price

2. What time did Communications Technician Johnson receive the call? 2.____
    _____ A.M.

    A. 10:00   B. 10:15   C. 10:20   D. 10:25

3. Which tenant was away on vacation? 3.____
    The tenant in Apartment

    A. 1C   B. IB   C. BI   D. ID

4. Dispatcher Watkins receives the following information regarding a complaint. 4.____
    Place of occurrence: St. James Park
    Complaint: Large group of intoxicated males throwing beer bottles and playing loud music
    Complainant: Oscar Aker
    Complainant's Address: 13 St. James Square, Apt. 2B
    Dispatcher Watkins is not certain if this incident should be reported to 911 or Mr. Aker's local precinct. Dispatcher Watkins is about to notify his supervisor of the call. Which one of the following expresses the above information MOST clearly and accurately?

A. Mr. Aker, who lives at 13 St. James Square, Apt. 2B, called to make a complaint of a large group of intoxicated males who are throwing beer bottles and playing loud music in St. James Park.

B. Mr. Aker, who lives at 13 St. James Square, called to complain about a large group of intoxicated males, in Apt. 2B. They are throwing beer bottles and playing loud music in St. James Park.

C. Mr. Aker of 13 St. James Square, Apt. 2B, called to complain about loud music. There were a large group of intoxicated males throwing beer bottles in St. James Park.

D. As a result of intoxicated males throwing beer bottles Mr. Aker of 13 St. James Square, Apt. 2B, called to complain. A large group was playing loud music in St. James Park.

5. Communications Operator Davis recorded the following information from a caller: 5.____

Crime:	Rape
Time of Rape:	11:30 A.M.
Place of Rape:	Ralph's Dress Shop, 200 Lexington
Avenue Victim:	Linda Castro - employee at Ralph's Dress Shop
Description of Suspect:	Male, white
Weapon:	Knife

Communications Operator Davis needs to be clear and accurate when relaying information to the patrol car. Which one of the following expresses the above information MOST clearly and accurately?

A. Linda Castro was at 200 Lexington Avenue when she was raped at knife point by a white male. At 11:30 A.M., she is an employee of Ralph's Dress Shop.

B. At 11:30 A.M., Linda Castro reported that she was working in Ralph's Dress Shop located at 200 Lexington Avenue. A white male raped her while she was working at knife point.

C. Linda Castro, an employee of Ralph's Dress Shop, located at 200 Lexington Avenue, reported that at 11:30 A.M. a white male raped her at knife point in the dress shop.

D. At 11:30 A.M., a white male pointed a knife at Linda Castro. He raped an employee of Ralph's Dress Shop, which is located at 200 Lexington Avenue.

Question 6.

DIRECTIONS: Question 6 is to be answered SOLELY on the basis of the following information.

Police Communications Technicians frequently receive low priority calls, which are calls that do not require an immediate police response. When a low priority call is received, the Police Communications Technician should transfer the caller to a tape-recorded message which states *there will be a delay in police response.*

6. Police Communications Technicians should transfer to the low priority taped message a   6.____
call reporting a

A. hubcap missing from an auto
B. child has just swallowed poison

C. group of youths fighting with knives
D. woman being assaulted

Questions 7-9.

DIRECTIONS: Questions 7 through 9 are to be answered SOLELY on the basis of the following passage.

On Tuesday, March 20 at 11:55 P.M., Dispatcher Uzel receives a call from a female stating that she immediately needs the police. The dispatcher asks the caller for her address. The excited female answers, *I can not think of it right now*. The dispatcher tries to calm down the caller. At this point, the female caller tells the dispatcher that her address is 1934 Bedford Avenue. The caller then realizes that 1934 Bedford Avenue is her mother's address and gives her address as 3455 Bedford Avenue. Dispatcher Uzel enters the address into the computer and tells the caller that the cross streets are Myrtle and Willoughby Avenues. The caller answers, *I don't live near Willoughby Avenue*. The dispatcher repeats her address at 3455 Bedford Avenue. Then the female states that her name is Linda Harris and her correct address is 5534 Bedford Avenue. Dispatcher Uzel enters the new address into the computer and determines the cross streets to be Utica Avenue and Kings Highway. The caller agrees that these are the cross streets where she lives.

7. What is the caller's CORRECT address?   7.____

    A. Unknown   B. 1934 Bedford Avenue
    C. 3455 Bedford Avenue   D. 5534 Bedford Avenue

8. What are the cross streets of the correct address?   8.____

    A. Myrtle Avenue and Willoughby Avenue
    B. Utica Avenue and Kings Highway
    C. Bedford Avenue and Myrtle Avenue
    D. Utica Avenue and Willoughby Avenue

9. Why did the female caller telephone Dispatcher Uzel?   9.____

    A. She needed the cross streets for her address.
    B. Her mother needed assistance.
    C. The purpose of the call was not mentioned.
    D. She did not know where she lived.

Question 10.

DIRECTIONS: Question 10 is to be answered SOLELY on the basis of the following information.
When performing vehicle license plate checks, Operators should do the following in the order given:
    I. Request the license plate in question.
    II. Repeat the license plate back to the patrol car officers.
    III. Check the license plate locally in the computer.
    IV. Advise the patrol car officers of the results of the local check.
    V. Check the license plate nationally in the computer.
    VI. Advise the patrol car officers of the results of the nationwide check.

10. Operator Johnson gets a request from a patrol car officer for a license plate check on a suspicious car. The patrol car officer tells Operator Johnson that the license plate number is XYZ-843, which Operator Johnson repeats back to the patrol car officer. Operator Johnson checks the license plate locally and determines that the car was stolen in the New York City area.
What should Operator Johnson do NEXT?

    A. Repeat the license plate back to patrol car officers.
    B. Check the license plate nationally.
    C. Advise the patrol car officers of the results of the local check.
    D. Advise the patrol ear officers of the results of the nationwide check.

10.____

11. Police Communications Technician Hughes receives a call from the owner of The Diamond Dome Jewelry Store, reporting a robbery. He obtains the following information from the caller:

Place of Occurrence: The Diamond Dome Jewelry Store, 10 Exchange Place
Time of Occurrence: 10:00 A.M.
Crime: Robbery of a $50,000 diamond ring
Victim: Clayton Pelt, owner of The Diamond Dome Jewelry Store
Description of Suspect: Male, white, black hair, blue suit and gray shirt
Weapon: Gun

Communications Technician Hughes is about to relay the information to the dispatcher. Which one of the following expresses the above information MOST clearly and accurately?

    A. Clayton Pelt reported that at 10:00 A.M. his store, The Diamond Dome Jewelry Store, was robbed at gunpoint. At 10 Exchange Place, a white male with black hair took a $50,000 diamond ring. He was wearing a blue suit and gray shirt.
    B. At 10:00 A.M., a black-haired male robbed a $50,000 diamond ring from The Diamond Dome Jewelry Store, which is owned by Clayton Pelt. A white male was wearing a blue suit and gray shirt and had a gun at 10 Exchange Place.
    C. At 10:00 A.M., Clayton Pelt, owner of The Diamond Dome Jewelry Store, which is located at 10 Exchange Place, was robbed of a $50,000 diamond ring at gunpoint. The suspect is a white male with black hair wearing a blue suit and gray shirt.
    D. In a robbery that occurred at gunpoint, a white male with black hair robbed The Diamond Dome Jewelry Store, which is located at 10 Exchange Place. Clayton Pelt, the owner who was robbed of a $50,000 diamond ring, said he was wearing a blue suit and a gray shirt at 10:00 A.M.

11.____

12. Dispatcher Sanders receives the following information from the computer: Place of Occurrence: Bushwick Housing Projects, rear of Building 12B

Time of Occurrence: 6:00 P.M.
Crime: Mugging
Victim: Hispanic female
Suspect: Unknown

Dispatcher sanders is about to relay the information to the patrol car.
Which one of the following expresses the above information MOST clearly and accurately?

12.____

A. In the rear of Building 12B, a Hispanic female was mugged. An unknown suspect was in the Bushwick Housing Projects at 6:00 P.M.
B. At 6:00 P.M., a Hispanic female was mugged by an unknown suspect in the rear of Building 12B, in the Bushwick Housing Projects.
C. At 6:00 P.M., a female is in the rear of Building 12B in the Bushwick Housing Projects. An unknown suspect mugged a Hispanic female.
D. A suspect's identity is unknown in the rear of Building 12B in the Bushwick Housing Project at 6:00 P.M. A Hispanic female was mugged.

Questions 13-15.

DIRECTIONS: Questions 13 through 15 are to be answered SOLELY on the basis of the following passage.

Dispatcher Clark, who is performing a 7:30 A.M. to 3:30 P.M. tour of duty, receives a call from Mrs. Gold. Mrs. Gold states there are four people selling drugs in front of Joe's Cleaners, located at the intersection of Main Street and Broadway. After checking the location in the computer, Dispatcher Clark asks the caller to give a description of each person. She gives the following descriptions: one white male wearing a yellow shirt, green pants, and red sneakers; one Hispanic male wearing a red and white shirt, black pants, and white sneakers; one black female wearing a green and red striped dress and red sandals; and one black male wearing a green shirt, yellow pants, and green sneakers. She also states that the Hispanic male, who is standing near a blue van, has the drugs inside a small black shoulder bag. She further states that she saw the black female hide a gun inside a brown paper bag and place it under a black car parked in front of Joe's Cleaners. The drug selling goes on everyday at various times. During the week, it occurs from 7 A.M. to 1 P.M. and from 5 P.M. to 12 A.M., but on weekends it occurs from 3 P.M. until 7 A.M.

13. Which person was wearing red sneakers?   13._____

    A. Black male   B. Hispanic male
    C. Black female   D. White male

14. Mrs. Gold stated the drugs were located   14._____

    A. under the blue van
    B. inside the black shoulder bag
    C. under the black car
    D. inside the brown paper bag

15. At what time does Mrs. Gold state the drugs are sold on weekends?   15._____

    A. 7:30 A.M. - 3:30 P.M.   B. 7:00 A.M. - 1:00 P.M.
    C. 5:00 P.M. - 12:00 A.M.   D. 3:00 P.M. - 7:00 A.M.

16. Police Communications Technician Bentley receives a call of an auto being stripped. He   16._____
     obtains the following information from the caller:
     Place of Occurrence: Corner of West End Avenue and W. 72nd Street
     Time of Occurrence: 10:30 P.M.
     Witness: Mr. Simpson
     Suspects: Two white males
     Crime: Auto stripping
     Action Taken: Suspects fled before police arrived

Communications Technician Bentley is about to enter the incident into the computer and send the information to the dispatcher.

Which one of the following expresses the above information MOST clearly and accurately?

A. At 10:30 P.M., Mr. Simpson witnessed two white males stripping an auto parked at the corner of West End Avenue and W. 72nd Street. The suspects fled before the police arrived.

B. An auto was parked at the corner of West End Avenue and W. 72nd Street. Two white males who were stripping at 10:30 P.M. were witnessed by Mr. Simpson. Before the police arrived, the suspects fled.

C. Mr. Simpson saw two white males at the corner of West End Avenue and W. 72nd Street. Fleeing the scene before the police arrived, the witness saw the suspects strip an auto.

D. Before the police arrived at 10:30 P.M. on the corner of West End Avenue and W. 72nd Street, Mr. Simpson witnessed two white males. The suspects, who stripped an auto, fled the scene.

17. 911 Operator Washington receives a call of a robbery and obtains the following information regarding the incident:

Place of Occurrence:	First National Bank, 45 West 96th Street
Time of Occurrence:	2:55 P.M.
Amount Taken:	$10,000
Description of Suspect:	Male, black, wearing a leather jacket, blue jeans, and white shirt
Weapon:	Gun

911 Operator Washington is about to enter the call into the computer.

Which one of the following expresses the above information MOST clearly and accurately?

A. At 2:55 P.M., the First National Bank, located at 45 West 96th Street, was robbed at gunpoint of $10,000. The suspect is a black male and is wearing a leather jacket, blue jeans, and a white shirt.

B. Ten thousand dollars was robbed from the First National Bank at 2:55 P.M. A black male was wearing a leather jacket, blue jeans, and a white shirt at 45 West 96th Street. He also had a gun.

C. At 2:55 P.M., a male was wearing a leather jacket, blue jeans, and a white shirt. The First National Bank located at 45 West 96th Street was robbed by a black male. Ten thousand dollars was taken at gunpoint.

D. Robbing the First National Bank, a male wore a leather jacket, blue jeans, and a white shirt at gunpoint. A black male was at 45 W. 96th Street. At 2:55 P.M., $10,000 was taken.

17.___

Questions 18-20.

DIRECTIONS: Questions 18 through 20 are to be answered SOLELY on the basis of the following passage.

Police Communications Technician Gordon receives a call from a male stating there is a bomb set to explode in the gym of Public School 85 in two hours. Realizing the urgency of the call, the Communications Technician calls the radio dispatcher, who assigns Patrol Car 43A to the scene. Communications Technician Gordon then notifies her supervisor, Miss Smith, who first reviews the tape of the call, then calls the Operations Unit which is notified of all serious incidents, and she reports the facts. The Operations Unit notifies the Mayor's Information Agency and Borough Headquarters of the emergency situation.

18. Who did Communications Technician Gordon notify FIRST?   18._____

    A. Supervisor Smith   B. Operations Unit
    C. Patrol Car 43A   D. Radio dispatcher

19. The Operations Unit was notified   19._____

    A. to inform school personnel of the bomb
    B. so they can arrive at the scene before the bomb is scheduled to go off
    C. to evacuate the school
    D. due to the seriousness of the incident

20. Who did Miss Smith notify?   20._____

    A. Patrol Car 43A
    B. Operations Unit
    C. Mayor's Information Agency
    D. Borough Headquarters

KEY (CORRECT ANSWERS)

1.	D		11.	C
2.	C		12.	B
3.	A		13.	D
4.	A		14.	B
5.	C		15.	D
6.	A		16.	A
7.	D		17.	A
8.	B		18.	D
9.	C		19.	D
10.	C		20.	B

TEST 2

DIRECTIONS: Each question or incomplete statement is followed by several suggested answers or completions. Select the one that BEST answers the question or completes the statement. *PRINT THE LETTER OF THE CORRECT ANSWER IN THE SPACE AT THE RIGHT.*

1. A Police Communications Technician receives a call reporting a large gathering. She obtained the following information:

Place of Occurrence: Cooper Square Park
Time of Occurrence: 1:15 A.M.
Occurrence: Youths drinking and playing loud music
Complainant: Mrs. Tucker, 20 Cooper Square
Action Taken: Police scattered the crowd

Communications Technician Carter is about to relay the information to the dispatcher. Which one of the following expresses the above information MOST clearly and accurately?

    A. The police responded to Cooper Square Park because Mrs. Tucker, who called 911, lives at 20 Cooper Square. The group of youths was scattered due to drinking and playing loud music at 1:15 A.M.
    B. Mrs. Tucker, who lives at 20 Cooper Square, called 911 to make a complaint of a group of youths who were drinking and playing loud music in Cooper Square Park at 1:15 A.M. The police responded and scattered the crowd.
    C. Loud music and drinking in Cooper Square Park by a group of youths caused the police to respond and scatter the crowd. Mrs. Tucker called 911 and complained. At 1:15 A.M., she lives at 20 Cooper Square.
    D. Playing loud music and drinking, Mrs. Tucker called the police. The police scattered a group of youths in Cooper Square Park at 1:15 A.M. Mrs. Tucker lives at 20 Cooper Square.

2. Dispatcher Weston received a call from the owner of a gas station and obtained the following information:

Place of Occurrence: Blin's Gas Station, 1800 White Plains Road
Time of Occurrence: 10:30 A.M.
Occurrence: Left station without paying
Witness: David Perilli
Description of Auto: A white Firebird, license plate GEB275
Suspect: Male, white, wearing blue jeans and a black T-shirt

Dispatcher Weston is about to enter the information into the computer. Which one of the following expresses the above information MOST clearly and accurately?

    A. At 10:30 A.M., David Perilli witnessed a white male wearing blue jeans and a black T-shirt leave Blin's Gas Station, located at 1800 White Plains Road, without paying. The suspect was driving a white Firebird with license plate GEB275.
    B. Wearing blue jeans and a black T-shirt, David Perilli witnessed a white male leave Blin's Gas Station without paying. He was driving a white Firebird with license plate GEB275. This occurred at 1800 White Plains Road at 10:30 A.M.
    C. David Perilli witnessed a male wearing blue jeans and a black T-shirt driving a white Firebird. At 10:30 A.M., a white male left Blin's Gas Station, located at 1800 White Plains Road, without paying. His license plate was GEB275.

1.____

2.____

D. At 10:30 A.M., David Perilli witnessed a white male leaving Blin's Gas Station without paying. The driver of a white Firebird, license plate GEB275, was wearing blue jeans and a black T-shirt at 1800 White Plains Road.

Questions 3-4.

DIRECTIONS: Questions 3 and 4 are to be answered SOLELY on the basis of the following information.

Police Communications Technicians are required to assist callers who need non-emergency assistance. The callers are referred to non-emergency agencies. Listed below are some non-emergency situations and the agencies to which they should be referred.

Agency
Local Precinct   Unoccupied suspicious car
Environmental Protection Agency   Open fire hydrant
Sanitation Department   Abandoned car
S.P.C.A.   Injured, stray or sick animal
Transit Authority   Transit Authority travel information

3. Communications Technician Carter received a call from Mr. Cane, who stated that a car without license plates had been parked in front of his house for five days. Mr. Crane should be referred to the

3.____

A. A.S.P.C.A.
B. Transit Authority
C. Sanitation Department
D. Environmental Protection Agency

4. Mrs. Dunbar calls to report that a dog has been hit by a car and is lying at the curb in front of her house. Mrs. Dunbar should be referred to the

4.____

A. Sanitation Department
B. Local Precinct
C. Environmental Protection Agency
D. A.S.P.C.A.

5. Operator Bryant received a call of a robbery and obtained the following information:

5.____

Place of Occurrence: Deluxe Deli, 303 E. 30th Street
Time of Occurrence: 5:00 P.M.
Crime: Robbery of $300
Victim: Bonnie Smith, cashier of Deluxe Deli
Description of Suspect: White, female, blonde hair, wearing black slacks and a red shirt
Weapon: Knife

Operator Bryant is about to enter this information into the computer.
Which one of the following expresses the above information MOST clearly and accurately?

A. Bonnie Smith, the cashier of the Deluxe Deli reported at 5:00 P.M. that she was robbed of $300 at knifepoint at 303 East 30th Street. A white female with blonde hair was wearing black slacks and a red shirt.

B. At 5:00 P.M., a blonde-haired female robbed the 303 East 30th Street store. At the Deluxe Deli, cashier Bonnie Smith was robbed of $300 by a white female at knifepoint. She was wearing black slacks and a red shirt.

C. In a robbery that occurred at knifepoint, a blonde-haired white female robbed $300 from the Deluxe Deli. Bonnie Smith, cashier of the 303 East 30th Street store, said she was wearing black slacks and a red shirt at 5:00 P.M.

D. At 5:00 P.M., Bonnie Smith, cashier of the Deluxe Deli, located at 303 East 30th Street, was robbed of $300 at knifepoint. The suspect is a white female with blonde hair wearing black slacks and a red shirt.

6. 911 Operator Landers receives a call reporting a burglary that happened in the past. He obtained the following information from the caller:

Place of Occurrence:	196 Simpson Street
Date of Occurrence:	June 12
Time of Occurrence:	Between 8:30 A.M. and 7:45 P.M.
Victim:	Mr. Arnold Frank
Items Stolen:	$300 cash, stereo, assorted jewelry, and a VCR

911 Operator Landers is about to enter the incident into the computer.
Which one of the following expresses the above information MOST clearly and accurately?

6.___

A. Mr. Arnold Frank stated that on June 12, between 8:30 A.M. and 7:45 P.M., someone broke into his home at 196 Simpson Street and took $300 in cash, a stereo, assorted jewelry, and a VCR.

B. Mr. Arnold Frank stated between 8:30 A.M. and 7:45 P.M., he lives at 196 Simpson Street. A stereo, VCR, $300 in cash, and assorted jewelry were taken on June 12.

C. Between 8:30 A.M. and 7:45 P.M. on June 12, Mr. Arnold Frank reported someone broke into his home. At 196 Simpson Street, a VCR, $300 in cash, a stereo, and assorted jewelry were taken.

D. A stereo, VCR, $300 in cash, and assorted jewelry were taken between 8:30 M. and 7:45 P.M. On June 12, Mr. Arnold Frank reported he lives at 196 Simpson Street.

Questions 7-9.

DIRECTIONS: Questions 7 through 9 are to be answered SOLELY on the basis of the following passage.

Communications Operator Harris receives a call from Mrs. Stein who reports that a car accident occurred in front of her home. She states that one of the cars belongs to her neighbor, Mrs. Brown, and the other car belongs to Mrs. Stein's son, Joseph Stein. Communications Operator Harris enters Mrs. Stein's address into the computer and receives information that no such address exists. She asks Mrs. Stein to repeat her address. Mrs. Stein repeats her address and states that gasoline is leaking from the cars and that smoke is coming from their engines. She further states that people are trapped in the cars and then hangs up.

Communications Operator Harris notifies her supervisor, Jones, that she received a call but was unable to verify the address and that the caller hung up. Mrs. Jones listens to the tape of the call and finds that the caller stated 450 Park Place not 415 Park Place. She advises Communications Operator Harris to enter the correct address, then notify Emergency Service Unit to respond to the individuals trapped in the cars, the Fire Department for the smoke condition, and Emergency Medical Service for any possible injuries.

7. Who did Communications Operator Harris notify concerning the problem with the caller's address?   7._____

    A. Mrs. Brown   B. Joseph Stein
    C. Joseph Brown   D. Mrs. Jones

8. Which agency was Communications Operator Harris advised to notify concerning individuals trapped in the cars?   8._____

    A. Emergency Medical Service
    B. Fire Department
    C. Emergency Service Unit
    D. NYC Police Department

9. Which agency did Supervisor Jones advise Communications Operator Harris to notify for the smoke condition?   9._____

    A. NYC Police Department
    B. Emergency Medical Service
    C. Fire Department
    D. Emergency Service Unit

Question 10.

DIRECTIONS: Question 10 is to be answered SOLELY on the basis of the following information:

When a Police Communications Technician receives a call concerning a bank robbery, a Communications Technician should do the following in the order given:

     I.   Get address and name of the bank from the caller.
    II. Enter the address into the computer.
   III. Use the *Hotline* button to alert the dispatcher of the serious incident going into the computer.
   IV. Get back to the caller and get the description of the suspect and other pertinent information.
    V. Enter additional information into the computer and send it to the dispatcher.
   VI. Upgrade the seriousness of the incident so it appears first on dispatcher's screen.
  VII. Notify the Supervising Police Communications Technician of the bank robbery.

10. Police Communications Technician Brent receives a call from Mr. Ross stating that while   10.____
he was on line at the Trust Bank, at West 34th Street and 9th Avenue, he witnessed a
bank robbery. Communications Technician Brent enters the address into the computer,
then presses the *Hotline* button and alerts the dispatcher that there was a bank robbery
at the Trust Bank on West 34th Street and 9th Avenue. Mr. Ross continues to state that
the robber is a white male in his 30's wearing a light blue shirt and blue jeans.
After obtaining other pertinent information, the NEXT step Communications Technician
Brent should take is to

   A.   enter additional information into the computer and send it to the dispatcher
   B.   upgrade the seriousness of the incident so it appears first on the dispatcher's
        screen
   C.   notify his supervisor of the bank robbery
   D.   use the *Hotline* button to alert the dispatcher of a serious incident going into the
        computer

11. Dispatcher Wilson receives a call regarding drugs being sold in the lobby of an apart-   11.____
ment building. He obtains the following information:

Place of Occurrence: 305 Willis Avenue
Time of Occurrence: 2:00 P.M.
Witnesses: Roy Rodriguez and Harry Armstrong
Suspect: Melvin Talbot, left the scene before the police arrived
Crime: Drug sale

Dispatcher Wilson is about to enter this incident into the computer.
Which one of the following expresses the above information MOST clearly and accurately?

   A.   Roy Rodriguez and Harry Armstrong reported that they witnessed Melvin Talbot
        selling drugs in the lobby of 305 Willis Avenue at 2:00 P.M. The suspect left the
        scene before the police arrived.
   B.   In the lobby, Roy Rodriguez reported at 2:00 P.M. he saw Melvin Talbot selling
        drugs with Harry Armstrong. He left the lobby of 305 Willis Avenue before the
        police arrived.
   C.   Roy Rodriguez and Harry Armstrong witnessed drugs being sold at 305 Willis Ave-
        nue. Before the police arrived at 2:00 P.M., Melvin Talbot left the lobby.
   D.   Before the police arrived, witnesses stated that Melvin Talbot was selling drugs. At
        305 Willis Avenue, in the lobby, Roy Rodriguez and Harry Armstrong said he left
        the scene at 2:00 P.M.

12. Operator Rogers receives a call of a car being stolen. He obtains the following informa-   12.____
tion:

Place of Occurrence: Parking lot at 1723 East 20th Street
Time of Occurrence: 2:30 A.M.
Vehicle Involved: 1988 Toyota Corolla
Suspects: Male, Hispanic, wearing a red T-shirt
Crime: Auto theft
Witness: Janet Alonzo

Operator Rogers is entering the information into the computer.
Which one of the following expresses the above information MOST clearly and accurately?

A. At 2:30 A.M., wearing a red T-shirt, Janet Alonzo witnessed a 1988 Toyota Corolla being stolen by a male Hispanic in the parking lot at 1723 East 20th Street.
B. A male Hispanic, wearing a red T-shirt, was in the parking lot at 1723 East 20th Street." At 2:30 A.M., Janet Alonzo witnessed a 1988 Toyota Corolla being stolen.
C. At 2:30 A.M., Janet Alonzo witnessed a 1988 Toyota Corolla in the parking lot at 1723 East 20th Street being stolen by a male Hispanic who is wearing a red T-shirt.
D. Janet Alonzo witnessed a 1988 Toyota Corolla in the parking lot being stolen. At 2:30 A.M., a male Hispanic was wearing a red T-shirt at 1723 East 20th Street.

Question 13.

DIRECTIONS: Question 13 is to be answered SOLELY on the basis of the following information.

There are times when Police Communications Technicians have to reassign officers in a patrol car from a less serious incident which does not require immediate police response to an incident of a more serious nature which does require immediate police response. Police Communications Technicians must choose among the assigned patrol cars and determine which one is assigned to the least serious incident, then reassign that one to the situation which requires immediate police response.

Communications Technician Reese is working the 13th Division which covers the 79th Precinct. There are only four patrol cars working in the 79th Precinct. They are assigned as follows:

79A is assigned to a car accident with injuries involving an intoxicated driver.

79B is assigned to a group of teenagers playing loud music in a park.

79C is assigned to a group of teenagers trying to steal liquor in a liquor store, who are possibly armed with guns.

79D is assigned to a suspicious man in a bank, with possible intentions to rob the bank.

13. If Communications Technician Reese receives a call of an incident that requires immediate police response, which patrol car should be reassigned?   13._____

A. 79A   B. 79B   C. 79C   D. 79D

Questions 14-16.

DIRECTIONS: Questions 14 through 16 are to be answered SOLELY on the basis of the following information.

On May 12, at 3:35 P.M., Police Communications Technician Connor receives a call from a child caller requesting an ambulance for her mother, whom she cannot wake. The child did not know her address, but gave Communications Technician Connor her apartment number and telephone number. Communications Technician Connor's supervisor, Ms. Bendel, is advised of the situation and consult's Cole's Directory, a listing published by the Bell Telephone Company, to obtain an address when only the telephone number is known. The telephone number is unlisted. Ms. Bendel asks Communications Technician Taylor to call Telco Security to obtain an address from their telephone number listing. Communications Technician Taylor speaks to Ms. Morris of Telco Security and obtains the address. Communications Technician Connor, who is still talking with the child, is given the address by Communications Technician Taylor. She enters the information into the computer system and transfers the caller to the Emergency Medical Service.

14. What information did Communications Technician Connor obtain from the child caller?　14.____

    A.　Telephone number and apartment number
    B.　Name and address
    C.　Address and telephone number
    D.　Apartment number and address

15. Communications Technician Taylor obtained the address from　15.____

    A.　Communications Technician Connor
    B.　Ms. Morris
    C.　Supervisor Bendel
    D.　the child caller

16. The caller's address was obtained by calling　16.____

    A.　Cole's Directory
    B.　Telco Security
    C.　Emergency Medical Service
    D.　The Telephone Company

Question 17.

DIRECTIONS:　Question 17 is to be answered SOLELY on the basis of the following information.

The following incidents appear on the Police Communications Technician's computer screen which were called in by three different callers at the same time:

    I.　At 3040 Hill Avenue between Worth and Centre Streets, there are two people fighting in the third floor hallway. One of them has a shiny metal object.
    II.　In a building located on Hill Avenue between Worth and Centre Streets, a man and a woman are having an argument on the third floor. The woman has a knife in her hand.
    III.　In front of Apartment 3C on the third floor, a husband and wife are yelling at each other. The wife is pointing a metal letter opener at her husband. The building is located on the corner of Hill Avenue and Worth Street.

17. A Police Communications Technician may be required to combine into one incident many　17.____
calls that appear on the computer screen if they seem to be reporting the same incident. Which of the above should a Police Communications Technician combine into one incident?

    A.　I and II   B.　I and III
    C.　II and III   D.　I, II, and III

Questions 18-19.

DIRECTIONS: Questions 18 and 19 are to be answered SOLELY on the basis of the following
                information.

Police Communications Technicians must be able to identify and assign codes to the
crimes described in the calls they receive. All crimes are coded by number and by priority. The
priority code number indicates the seriousness of the crime. The lower the priority number, the
more serious the crime.

Listed below is a chart of several crimes and their definitions. The corresponding crime
code and priority code number are given.

CRIME	DEFINITION	CRIME CODE	PRIORITY CODE
Criminal Mischief:	Occurs when a person intentionally damages another person's property	29	6
Harrassment:	Occurs when a person intentionally annoys another person by striking, shoving, or kicking them without causing injury	27	8
Aggravated Harrassment:	Occurs when a person intentionally annoys another person by using any form of communication	28	9
Theft of Service:	Occurs when a person intentionally avoids payment for services given	25	7

18. Communications Technician Rogers received a call from Mrs. Freeman, who stated that   18._____
     her next door neighbor, whom she had an argument with, has thrown a rock through her
     apartment window.
     Which one of the following is the CORRECT crime code?

     A. 29   B. 28   C. 27   D. 25

19. Communications Technician Tucker received a call from a man who stated that he is a   19._____
     waiter at the Frontier Diner. He states that one of his customers was refusing to pay for
     his meal.
     Which one of the following is the CORRECT priority code number for this crime?

     A. 6   B. 7   C. 8   D. 9

Dispatcher Matthews received a call of a bomb threat. He obtained the following infor-   19._____
mation;
Address of Occurrence: 202 Church Avenue
Location: 2nd floor men's room
Time of Call: 12:00 P.M.
Time of Occurrence: 2:00 P.M.
Terrorist Organization: People *Against Government*

Caller: Anonymous male member of *People* Against Government
Action Taken: Supervisor Jones notified of the bomb threat
Dispatcher Matthews is about to enter the information into the computer.
Which one of the following expresses the above information MOST clearly and accurately?

A. An anonymous male called Dispatcher Matthews and told him that a bomb is set to go off at 202 Church Avenue in the 2nd floor men's room at 2:00 P.M. Dispatcher Matthews notified Supervisor Jones that the caller is from *People Against Government* at 12:00 P.M.

B. Dispatcher Matthews received a call in the 2nd floor men's room of a bomb threat from an anonymous male member of the *People Against Government* terrorist organization. He notified Supervisor Jones at 12:00 P.M. that a bomb is set to go off at 2:00 P.M. at 202 Church Avenue.

C. Dispatcher Matthews received a call at 202 Church Avenue from the *People Against Government,* a terrorist organization. An anonymous male stated that a bomb is set to go off at 2:00 P.M. in the 2nd floor men's room. At 12:00 P.M., Dispatcher Matthews notified Supervisor Jones of the call.

D. At 12:00 P.M., Dispatcher Matthews received a call from an anonymous male caller who states that he is from a terrorist organization known as *People Against Government*. He states that a bomb has been placed in the 2nd floor men's room of 202 Church Avenue and is set to go off at 2:00 P.M. Dispatcher Matthews notified Supervisor Jones of the bomb threat.

KEY (CORRECT ANSWERS)

1.	B		11.	A
2.	A		12.	C
3.	C		13.	B
4.	D		14.	A
5.	D		15.	B
6.	A		16.	B
7.	D		17.	D
8.	C		18.	A
9.	C		19.	B
10.	A		20.	D

EXAMINATION SECTION
TEST 1

DIRECTIONS: Each question or incomplete statement is followed by several suggested answers or completions. Select the one that BEST answers the question or completes the statement. *PRINT THE LETTER OF THE CORRECT ANSWER IN THE SPACE AT THE RIGHT.*

1. You are operating the switchboard and you receive an outside call for an extension line which is busy.
   The one of the following which you should do FIRST is to

   A. ask the caller to try again later
   B. ask the caller to wait and inform him every thirty seconds about the status of the extension line
   C. tell the caller the line is busy and ask him if he wishes to wait
   D. tell the caller the line is busy and that you will connect him as soon as possible

   1._____

2. A person comes to your work area. He makes comments which make no sense, gives foolish opinions, and tells you that he has enemies who are after him. He appears to be mentally ill.
   Of the following, the FIRST action to take is to

   A. humor him by agreeing and sympathizing with him
   B. try to reason with him and point out that his fears or opinions are unfounded
   C. have him arrested immediately
   D. tell him to leave at once

   2._____

3. You are speaking with someone on the telephone who asks you a question which you cannot answer. You estimate that you can probably obtain the requested information in about five minutes.
   Of the following, the MOST appropriate course of action would be to tell the caller that

   A. the information will take a short while to obtain, and then ask her for her name and number so that you can call her back when you have the information
   B. the information is available now, but she should call back later
   C. you do not know the answer and refer her to another division you think might be of service
   D. she is being placed on *hold* and that you will be with her in about five minutes

   3._____

4. A person with a very heavy foreign accent comes to your work area and starts talking to you. He is very excited and is speaking too rapidly for you to understand what he is saying.
   Of the following, the FIRST action for you to take is to

   A. refer the person to your supervisor
   B. continue your work and ignore the person in the hope that he will be discouraged and leave the building
   C. ask or motion to the person to speak more slowly and have him repeat what he is trying to communicate
   D. assume that the person is making a complaint, tell him that his problem will be taken care of, and then go back to your work

   4._____

5. Assume that you are responsible for handling supplies. You notice that you are running low on a particular type of manila file folder exceptionally fast. You believe that someone in the precinct is taking the folders for other than official use.
In this situation, the one of the following that you should do FIRST is to

    A.   put up a notice stating that supplies have been disappearing and ask for the staff's cooperation in eliminating the problem
    B.   speak to your supervisor about the matter and let him decide on a course of action
    C.   watch the supply cabinet to determine who is taking the folders
    D.   ignore the situation and put in a requisition for additional folders

    5.___

6. One afternoon, several of the officers ask you to perform different tasks. Each task requires a half day of work. Each officer tells you that his assignment must be finished by 4 P.M. the next day.
Of the following, the BEST way to handle this situation is to

    A.   do the assignments as quickly as you can, in the order in which the officers handed them to you
    B.   do some work on each assignment in the order of the ranks of the assigning officers and hand in as much as you are able to finish
    C.   speak to your immediate supervisor in order to determine the priority of assignments
    D.   accept all four assignments but explain to the last officer that you may not be able to finish his job

    6.___

7. Every morning, several officers congregate around your work station during their breaks. You find their conversations very distracting.
The one of the following which you should do FIRST is to

    A.   ask them to cooperate with you by taking their breaks somewhere else
    B.   concentrate as best you can because their breaks do not last very long
    C.   reschedule your break to coincide with theirs
    D.   tell your supervisor that the officers are very uncooperative

    7.___

8. One evening when you are very busy, you answer the phone and find that you are speaking with one of the neighborhood cranks, an elderly man who constantly complains that his neighbors are noisy.
In this situation, the MOST appropriate action for you to take is to

    A.   hang up and go on with your work
    B.   note the complaint and process it in the usual way
    C.   tell the man that his complaint will be investigated and then forget about it
    D.   tell the man that you are very busy and ask him to call back later

    8.___

9. One morning you answer a telephone call for Lieutenant Jones, who is busy on another line. You inform the caller that Lieutenant Jones is on another line and this party says he will hold. After two minutes, Lieutenant Jones is still speaking on the first call.
Of the following, the FIRST thing for you to do is to

    A.   ask the second caller whether it is an emergency
    B.   signal Lieutenant Jones to let him know there is another call waiting for him
    C.   request that the second caller try again later
    D.   inform the second caller that Lieutenant Jones' line is still busy

    9.___

10. The files in your office have been overcrowded and difficult to work with since you started   10.____
    working there. One day your supervisor is transferred and another aide in your office
    decides to discard three drawers of the oldest materials.
    For him to take this action is

    A. *desirable;* it will facilitate handling the more active materials
    B. *undesirable;* no file should be removed from its point of origin
    C. *desirable;* there is no need to burden a new supervisor with unnecessary informa-
       tion
    D. *undesirable;* no file should be discarded without first noting what material has been
       discarded

11. You have been criticized by the lieutenant-in-charge because of spelling errors in some   11.____
    of your typing. You have only copied the reports as written, and you realize that the errors
    occurred in work given to you by Sergeant X.
    Of the following, the BEST way for you to handle this situation is to

    A. tell the lieutenant that the spelling errors are Sergeant X's, not yours, because they
       occur only when you type his reports
    B. tell the lieutenant that you only type the reports as given to you, without implicating
       anyone
    C. inform Sergeant X that you have been unjustly criticized because of his spelling
       errors and politely request that he be more careful in the future
    D. use a dictionary whenever you have doubt regarding spelling

12. You have recently found several items misfiled. You believe that this occurred because a   12.____
    new administrative aide in your section has been making mistakes.
    The BEST course of action for you to take is to

    A. refile the material and say nothing about it
    B. send your supervisor an anonymous note of complaint about the filing errors
    C. show the errors to the new administrative aide and tell him why they are errors in
       filing
    D. tell your supervisor that the new administrative aide makes a lot of errors in filing

13. One of your duties is to record information on a standard printed form regarding missing   13.____
    cars. One call you receive concerns a custom-built auto which has apparently been sto-
    len. There seems to be no place on the form for many of the details which the owner
    gives you.
    Of the following, the BEST way for you to obtain an adequate description of this car
    would be to

    A. complete the form as best you can and attach another sheet containing the addi-
       tional information the owner gives you
    B. complete the form as best you can and request that the owner submit a photo-
       graph of the missing car
    C. scrap the form since it is inadequate in this case and make out a report based on
       the information the owner gives you
    D. complete the form as best you can and ignore extraneous information that the form
       does not call for

14. One weekend, you develop a painful infection in one hand. You know that your typing   14.__
speed will be much slower than normal, and the likelihood of your making mistakes will
be increased.
Of the following, the BEST course of action for you to take in this situation is to

   A. report to work as scheduled and do your typing assignments as best you can with-
       out complaining
   B. report to work as scheduled and ask your co-workers to divide your typing assign-
       ments until your hand heals
   C. report to work as scheduled and ask your supervisor for non-typing assignments
       until your hand heals
   D. call in sick and remain on medical leave until your hand is completely healed so
       that you can perform your normal duties

15. When filling out a departmental form during an interview concerning a citizen complaint,   15.__
an administrative aide should know the purpose of each question that he asks the citizen.
For such information to be supplied by the department is

   A. *advisable,* because the aide may lose interest in the job if he is not fully informed
       about the questions he has to ask
   B. *inadvisable,* because the aide may reveal the true purpose of the questions to the
       citizens
   C. *advisable,* because the aide might otherwise record superficial or inadequate
       answers if he does not fully understand the questions
   D. *inadvisable,* because the information obtained through the form may be of little
       importance to the aide

16. Which one of the following is NOT a generally accepted rule of telephone etiquette for an   16.__
administrative aide?

   A. Answer the telephone as soon as possible after the first ring
   B. Speak in a louder than normal tone of voice, on the assumption that the caller is
       hard-of-hearing
   C. Have a pencil and paper ready at all times with which to make notes and take mes-
       sages
   D. Use the tone of your voice to give the caller the impression of cooperativeness and
       willingness to be of service

17. The one of the following which is the BEST reason for placing the date and time of   17.__
receipt of incoming mail is that this procedure

   A. aids the filing of correspondence in alphabetical order
   B. fixes responsibility for promptness in answering correspondence
   C. indicates that the mail has been checked for the presence of a return address
   D. makes it easier to distribute the mail in sequence

18. Which one of the following is the FIRST step that you should take when filing a document   18.____
    by subject?

    A. Arrange related documents by date with the latest date in front
    B. Check whether the document has been released for filing
    C. Cross-reference the document if necessary
    D. Determine the category under which the document will be filed

19. The one of the following which is NOT generally employed to keep track of frequently   19.____
    used material requiring future attention is a

    A. card tickler file
    B. dated follow-up folder
    C. periodic transferral of records
    D. signal folder

20. Assume that a newly appointed administrative aide arrives 15 minutes late for the start of   20.____
    his tour of duty. One of his co-workers tells him not to worry because he has signed him
    in on time. The co-worker assures him that he would be willing to cover for him anytime
    he is late and hopes the aide will do the same for him. The aide agrees to do so.
    This arrangement is

    A. *desirable;* it prevents both men from getting a record for tardiness
    B. *undesirable;* signing in for each other is dishonest
    C. *desirable;* cooperation among co-workers is an important factor in morale
    D. *undesirable;* they will get caught if one is held up in a lengthy delay

21. An administrative aide takes great pains to help a citizen who approaches him with a   21.____
    problem. The citizen thanks the aide curtly and without enthusiasm.
    Under these circumstances, it would be MOST courteous for the aide to

    A. tell the citizen he was glad to be of service
    B. ask the citizen to put the compliment into writing and send it to his supervisor
    C. tell the citizen just what pains he took to render this service so that the citizen will
       be fully aware of his efforts
    D. make no reply and ignore the citizen's remarks

22. Assume that your supervisor spends a week training you, a newly appointed administra-   22.____
    tive aide, to sort fingerprints for filing purposes. After doing this type of filing for several
    days, you get an idea which you believe would improve upon the method in use.
    Of the following, the BEST action for you to take in this situation is to

    A. wait to see whether your idea still looks good after you have had more experience
    B. try your idea out before bringing it up with your supervisor
    C. discuss your idea with your supervisor
    D. forget about this idea since the fingerprint sorting system was devised by experts

23. Which one of the following is NOT a useful filing practice?   23.____

    A. Filing active records in the most accessible parts of the file cabinet
    B. Filling a file drawer to capacity in order to save space
    C. Gluing small documents to standard-size paper before filing
    D. Using different colored labels for various filing categories

24. A citizen comes in to make a complaint to an administrative aide.   24.___
The one of the following actions which would be the MOST serious example of discourtesy would be for the aide to

    A. refuse to look up from his desk even though he knows someone is waiting to speak to him
    B. not use the citizen's name when addressing him once his identity has been ascertained
    C. interrupt the citizen's story to ask questions
    D. listen to the complaint and refer the citizen to a special office

25. Suppose that one of your neighbors walks into the precinct where you are an administra-   25.___
tive aide and asks you to make 100 copies of a letter on the office duplicating machine for his personal use.
Of the following, what action should you take FIRST in this situation?

    A. Pretend that you do not know the person and order him to leave the building
    B. Call a police officer and report the person for attempting to make illegal use of police equipment
    C. Tell the person that you will copy the letter but only when you are off duty
    D. Explain to the person that you cannot use police equipment for non-police work

---

KEY (CORRECT ANSWERS)

1.	C		11.	D
2.	A		12.	C
3.	A		13.	A
4.	C		14.	C
5.	B		15.	C
6.	C		16.	B
7.	A		17.	B
8.	B		18.	B
9.	D		19.	C
10.	D		20.	B

21.	A
22.	C
23.	B
24.	A
25.	D

TEST 2

DIRECTIONS: Each question or incomplete statement is followed by several suggested answers or completions. Select the one that BEST answers the question or completes the statement. *PRINT THE LETTER OF THE CORRECT ANSWER IN THE SPACE AT THE RIGHT.*

Questions 1-6.

DIRECTIONS: Questions 1 through 6 are to be answered on the basis of the information supplied in the chart below.

LAW ENFORCEMENT OFFICERS KILLED
(By Type of Activity)

1991-2000

LAW ENFORCEMENT OFFICERS KILLED
(By Type of Activity)

1991-1995 [   ]
1996-2000 [IIII]

Type of Activity	1991-1995	1996-2000
RESPONDING TO DISTURBANCE CALLS	48	50
BURGLARIES IN PROGRESS OR PURSUING BURGLARY SUSPECT	28	25
ROBBERIES IN PROGRESS OR PURSUING ROBBERY SUSPECT	48	74
ATTEMPTING OTHER ARRESTS	56	112
CIVIL DISORDERS	2	8
HANDLING, TRANSPORTING, CUSTODY OF PRISONERS	12	17
INVESTIGATING SUSPICIOUS PERSONS AND CIRCUMSTANCES	28	29
AMBUSH	13	29
UNPROVOKED MENTALLY DERANGED	5	20
TRAFFIC STOPS	10	19

1. According to the above chart, the percent of the total number of law enforcement officers killed from 1991-2000 in activities related to burglaries and robberies is MOST NEARLY _____ percent.

    A. 8.4   B. 19.3   C. 27.6   D. 36.2

1.__

2. According to the above chart, the two of the following categories which increased from 1991-95 to 1996-00 by the same percent are

    A. ambush and traffic stops
    B. attempting other arrests and ambush
    C. civil disorders and unprovoked mentally deranged
    D. response to disturbance calls and investigating suspicious persons and circumstances

2.__

3. According to the above chart, the percentage increase in law enforcement officers killed from the 1991-95 period to the 1996-00 period is MOST NEARLY _____ percent.

    A. 34   B. 53   C. 65   D. 100

3.__

4. According to the above chart, in which one of the following activities did the number of law enforcement officers killed increase by 100 percent?

    A. Ambush
    B. Attempting other arrests
    C. Robberies in progress or pursuing robbery suspect
    D. Traffic stops

4.__

5. According to the above chart, the two of the following activities during which the total number of law enforcement officers killed from 1991 to 2000 was the same are

    A. burglaries in progress or pursuing burglary suspect and investigating suspicious persons and circumstances
    B. handling, transporting, custody of prisoners and traffic stops
    C. investigating suspicious persons and circumstances and ambush
    D. responding to disturbance calls and robberies in progress or pursuing robbery suspect

5.__

6. According to the categories in the above chart, the one of the following statements which can be made about law enforcement officers killed from 1991 to 1995 is that

    A. the number of law enforcement officers killed during civil disorders equals one-sixth of the number killed responding to disturbance calls
    B. the number of law enforcement officers killed during robberies in progress or pursuing robbery suspect equals 25 percent of the number killed while handling or transporting prisoners
    C. the number of law enforcement officers killed during traffic stops equals one-half the number killed for unprovoked reasons or by the mentally deranged
    D. twice as many law enforcement officers were killed attempting other arrests as were killed during burglaries in progress or pursuing burglary suspect

6.__

Questions 7-10.

DIRECTIONS: Assume that all arrests fall into two mutually exclusive categories, felonies and misdemeanors. Last week 620 arrests were made in Precinct A, of which 403 were for felonies. Questions 7 through 10 are to be answered on the basis of this information.

7. The percent of all arrests made in Precinct A last week which were for felonies was _____ percent.

7.____

    A. 55   B. 60   C. 65   D. 70

8. If 3/5 of all persons arrested for felonies and 1/4 of all persons arrested for misdemeanors were carrying weapons, then the number of arrests involving persons carrying weapons in Precinct A last week was MOST NEARLY

8.____

    A. 135   B. 295   C. 415   D. 525

9. If five times as many men as women were arrested for felonies, and half as many women as men were arrested for misdemeanors, then the number of women arrested in Precinct A last week was APPROXIMATELY

9.____

    A. 90   B. 120   C. 175   D. 210

10. If the ratio of arrests made on weekends (Friday through Sunday) to arrests made on weekdays (Monday through Thursday) is 2:1, then the number of arrests made in . Precinct A last weekend was

10.____

    A. 308   B. 340   C. 372   D. 413

11. The police precincts covering the county receive calls at the average rate of two per minute during the 8 A.M. to 4 P.M. tour, but this rate increases by 50 percent during the 4 P.M. to 12 M. tour. However, the initial rate decreases by 50 percent during the 12 M. to 8 A.M. tour.
The number of calls received by the precincts covering the county on this basis in one 24-hour day is

11.____

    A. 960   B. 1440 ·   C. 2880   D. 3360

12. If an administrative aide is expected to handle 15 calls per hour and Precinct C averages 840 calls during the 4 P.M. to 12 M. tour, then the number of aides needed in Precinct C to handle calls during this tour is

12.____

    A. 4   B. 5   C. 6   D. 7

13. If in a group of ten administrative aides, four type 40 words per minute, one types 45, two type 50, two type 60, and one types 65, then the average speed in the group is _____ words per minute.

13.____

    A. 49   B. 50   C. 51   D. 52

14. An administrative aide works from midnight to 8 A.M. on a certain day and then is off for 64 hours.
He is due back at work at

14.____

    A. 8 A.M.   B. 12 noon
    C. 4 P.M.   D. 12 midnight

15. If a certain aide takes one hour to type 2 accident reports or 6 missing person reports, then the length of time he will require to finish 7 accident reports and 15 missing persons reports is _____ hours _____ minutes.   15.____

    A. 6; 0   B. 6; 30   C. 8; 0   D. 8; 40

16. If one administrative aide can alphabetize 320 reports per hour and another can do 280 per hour, then the number of reports that both could alphabetize during an 8-hour tour is   16.____

    A. 4800   B. 5200   C. 5400   D. 5700

17. If 1000 candidates applied for administrative aide, and out of those applying 7/8 appear for the written test, and out of those who take the written test 66 2/3 percent pass it, and out of those who pass the written test 85 percent pass the medical exam, then the number of candidates still eligible to become administrative aides will be about   17.____

    A. 245   B. 495   C. 585   D. 745

18. If the number of murders in the city in 1980 was 415, and the number of murders has increased by 8 percent each year since that year, then in 1983 we would expect the number of murders to be about   18.____

    A. 484   B. 523   C. 548   D. 565

19. If a person reported missing on April 15 was found murdered on July 4, how many days was he missing? (Include April 15 but NOT July 4 in the total.)   19.____

    A. 76   B. 80   C. 82   D. 84

20. Suppose that a pile of 96 file cards measures one inch in height and that it takes you 1/2 hour to file these cards away.   20.____
     If you are given three piles of cards which measure 2 1/2 inches high, 1 3/4 inches high, and 3 3/8 inches high, respectively, the time it would take to file the cards is MOST NEARLY _____ hours and _____ minutes.

    A. 2; 30   B. 3; 50   C. 6; 45   D. 8; 15

Questions 21-30.

DIRECTIONS: Questions 21 through 30 test how good you are at catching mistakes in typing or printing. In each question, the name and addresses in Column I should be an exact copy of the name and address in Column I.
Mark your answer
    A.   if there is no mistake in either name or address
    B.   if there is a mistake in both name and address
    C.   if there is a mistake only in the name
    D.   if there is a mistake only in the address

<u>COLUMN I</u>   <u>COLUMN II</u>

21. Milos Yanocek   Milos Yanocek   21.____
     33-60 14 Street   33-60 14 Street
     Long Island City, NY 11011   Long Island City, NY 11001

22.	Alphonse Sabattelo 24 Minnetta Lane New York, NY 10006	Alphonse Sabbattelo 24 Minetta Lane New York, NY 10006
23.	Helen Stearn 5 Metropolitan Oval Bronx, NY 10462	Helene Stearn 5 Metropolitan Oval Bronx, NY 10462
24.	Jacob Weisman 231 Francis Lewis Boulevard Forest Hills, NY 11325	Jacob Weisman 231 Francis Lewis Boulevard Forest Hill, NY 11325
25.	Riccardo Fuente 135 West 83 Street New York, NY 10024	Riccardo Fuentes 134 West 88 Street New York, NY 10024
26.	Dennis Lauber 52 Avenue D Brooklyn, NY 11216	Dennis Lauder 52 Avenue D Brooklyn, NY 11216
27.	Paul Cutter 195 Galloway Avenue Staten Island, NY 10356	Paul Cutter 175 Galloway Avenue Staten Island, NY 10365
28.	Sean Donnelly 45-58 41 Avenue Woodside, NY 11168	Sean Donnelly 45-58 41 Avenue Woodside, NY 11168
29.	Clyde Willot 1483 Rockaway Avenue Brooklyn, NY 11238	Clyde Willat 1483 Rockway Avenue Brooklyn, NY 11238
30.	Michael Stanakis 419 Sheriden Avenue Staten Island, NY 10363	Michael Stanakis 419 Sheraden Avenue Staten Island, NY 10363

Questions 31-40.

DIRECTIONS: Questions 31 through 40 are to be answered only on the basis of the following information.

Column I consists of serial numbers of dollar bills. Column II shows different ways of arranging the corresponding serial numbers.

The serial numbers of dollar bills in Column I begin and end with a capital letter and have an eight-digit number in between. The serial numbers in Column I are to be arranged according to the following rules:

First: In alphabetical order according to the first letter
Second: When two or more serial numbers have the same first letter, in alphabetical order according to the last letter

Third: When two or more serial numbers have the same first and last letters, in numerical order, beginning with the lowest number.

The serial numbers in Column I are numbered (1) through (5) in the order in which they are listed. In Column II, the numbers (1) through (5) are arranged in four different ways to show different arrangements of the corresponding serial numbers. Choose the answer in Column II in which the serial numbers are arranged according to the above rules.

SAMPLE QUESTION:

	COLUMN I		COLUMN II
(1)	E75044127B	(A)	4, 1, 3, 2, 5
(2)	B96399104A	(B)	4, 1, 2, 3,5
(3)	B93939086A	(C)	4,3, 2, 5,1
(4)	B47064465H	(D)	3, 2, 5, 4,1
(5)	B99040922A		

In the sample question, the four serial numbers starting with B should be put before the serial numbers starting with E. The serial numbers starting with B and ending with A should be put before the serial number starting with B and ending with H. The three serial numbers starting with B and ending with A should be listed in numerical order, beginning with the lowest number. The correct way to arrange the serial numbers, therefore, is

(3) B93939086A
(2) B96399104A
(5) B99040922A
(4) B47064465H
(1) E75044127B

Since the order of arrangement is 3, 2, 5, 4, 1, the answer to the sample question is (D).

        COLUMN I   COLUMN II

31. (1) P44343314Y   A. 2, 3, 1, 4, 5   31.__
      (2) P44141341S   B. 1, 5, 3, 2, 4
      (3) P44141431L   C. 4, 2, 3, 5, 1
      (4) P41143413W   D. 5, 3, 2, 4, 1
      (5) P44313433H

32. (1) D89077275M   A. 3, 2, 5, 3, 1   32.__
      (2) D98073724N   B. 1, 4, 3, 2, 5
      (3) D90877274N   C. 4, 1, 5, 2, 3
      (4) D98877275M   D. 1, 3, 2, 5, 3
      (5) D98873725N

33. (1) H32548137E   A. 2, 4, 5, 1, 3   33.__
      (2) H35243178A   B. 1, 5, 2, 3, 4
      (3) H35284378F   C. 1, 5, 2, 4, 3,
      (4) H35288337A   D. 2, 1, 5, 3, 4
      (5) H32883173B

34.   (1) K24165039H   A.   4, 2, 5, 3, 1   34.____
       (2) F24106599A   B.   2, 3, 4, 1, 5
       (3) L21406639G   C.   4, 2, 5, 1, 3
       (4) C24156093A   D.   1, 3, 4, 5, 2
       (5) K24165593D

35.   (1) H79110642E   A.   2, 1, 3, 5, 4   35.____
       (2) H79101928E   B.   2, 1, 4, 5, 3
       (3) A79111567F   C.   3, 5, 2, 1, 4
       (4) H79111796E   D.   4, 3, 5, 1, 2
       (5) A79111618F

36.   (1) P16388385W   A.   3, 4, 5, 2, 1   36.____
       (2) R16388335V   B.   2, 3, 4, 5, 1
       (3) P16383835W   C.   2, 4, 3, 1, 5
       (4) R18386865V   D.   3, 1, 5, 2, 4
       (5) P18686865W

37.   (1) B42271749G   A.   4, 1, 5, 2, 3   37.____
       (2) B42271779G   B.   4, 1, 2, 5, 3
       (3) E43217779G   C.   1, 2, 4, 5, 3
       (4) B42874119C   D.   5, 3, 1, 2, 4
       (5) E42817749G

38.   (1) M57906455S   A.   4, 1, 5, 3, 2   38.____
       (2) N87077758S   B.   3, 4, 1, 5, 2
       (3) N87707757B   C.   4, 1, 5, 2, 3
       (4) M57877759B   D.   1, 5, 3, 2, 4
       (5) M57906555S

39.   (1) C69336894Y   A.   2, 5, 3, 1, 4   39.____
       (2) C69336684V   B.   3, 2, 5, 1, 4
       (3) C69366887W   C.   3, 1, 4, 5, 2
       (4) C69366994Y   D.   2, 5, 1, 3, 4
       (5) C69336865V

40.   (1) A56247181D   A.   1, 5, 3, 2, 4   40.____
       (2) A56272128P   B.   3, 1, 5, 2, 4
       (3) H56247128D   C.   3, 2, 1, 5, 4
       (4) H56272288P   D.   1, 5, 2, 3, 4
       (5) A56247188D

Questions 41-48.

DIRECTIONS: Questions 41 through 48 are to be answered only on the basis of the following passage.

     Auto theft is prevalent and costly. In 1995, 486,000 autos valued at over $500 million were stolen. About 28 percent of the inhabitants of Federal prisons are there as a result of conviction of interstate auto theft under the Dyer Act. In California alone, auto thefts cost the criminal justice system approximately $60 million yearly.

The great majority of auto theft is for temporary use rather than resale, as evidenced by the fact that 88 percent of autos stolen in 1995 were recovered. In Los Angeles, 64 percent of stolen autos that were recovered were found within two days and about 80 percent within a week. Chicago reports that 71 percent of the recovered autos were found within four miles of the point of theft. The FBI estimates that 8 percent of stolen cars are taken for the purpose of stripping them for parts, 12 percent for resale, and 5 percent for use in another crime. Auto thefts are primarily juvenile acts. Although only 21 percent of all arrests for nontraffic offenses in 1995 were of individuals under 18 years of age, 63 percent of auto theft arrests were of persons under 18. Auto theft represents the start of many criminal careers; in an FBI sample of juvenile auto theft offenders, 41 percent had no prior arrest record.

41. In the passage above, the discussion of the reasons for auto theft does NOT include the percent of   41.___

    A. autos stolen by prior offenders
    B. recovered stolen autos found close to the point of theft
    C. stolen autos recovered within a week
    D. stolen autos which were recovered

42. Assuming the figures in the above passage remain constant, you may logically estimate the cost of auto thefts to the California criminal justice system over a five-year period beginning in 1995 to have been about _____ million.   42.___

    A. $200   B. $300   C. $440   D. $500

43. According to the above passage, the percent of stolen autos in Los Angeles which were not recovered within a week was _____ percent.   43.___

    A. 12   B. 20   C. 29   D. 36

44. According to the above passage, MOST auto thefts are committed by   44.___

    A. former inmates of Federal prisons
    B. juveniles
    C. persons with a prior arrest record
    D. residents of large cities

45. According to the above passage, MOST autos are stolen for   45.___

    A. resale   B. stripping of parts
    C. temporary use   D. use in another crime

46. According to the above passage, the percent of persons arrested for auto theft who were under 18   46.___

    A. equals nearly the same percent of stolen autos which were recovered
    B. equals nearly two-thirds of the total number of persons arrested for nontraffic offenses
    C. is the same as the percent of persons arrested for nontraffic offenses who were under 18
    D. is three times the percent of persons arrested for nontraffic offenses who were under 18

47. An APPROPRIATE title for the above passage is

    A. How Criminal Careers Begin
    B. Recovery of Stolen Cars
    C. Some Statistics on Auto Theft
    D. The Costs of Auto Theft

47._____

48. Based on the above passage, the number of cars taken for use in another crime in 1995 was

    A. 24,300   B. 38,880   C. 48,600   D. 58,320

48._____

Questions 49-55.

DIRECTIONS: Questions 49 through 55 are to be answered only on the basis of the following passage.

Burglar alarms are designed to detect intrusion automatically. Robbery alarms enable a victim of a robbery or an attack to signal for help. Such devices can be located in elevators, hallways, homes and apartments, businesses and factories, and subways, as well as on the street in high-crime areas. Alarms could deter some potential criminals from attacking targets so protected. If alarms were prevalent and not visible, then they might serve to suppress crime generally. In addition, of course, the alarms can summon the police when they are needed.

All alarms must perform three functions: sensing or initiation of the signal, transmission of the signal, and annunciation of the alarm. A burglar alarm needs a sensor to detect human presence or activity in an unoccupied enclosed area like a building or a room. A robbery victim would initiate the alarm by closing a foot or wall switch, or by triggering a portable transmitter which would send the alarm signal to a remote receiver. The signal can sound locally as a loud noise to frighten away a criminal, or it can be sent silently by wire to a central agency. A centralized annunciator requires either private lines from each alarmed point, or the transmission of some information on the location of the signal.

49. A conclusion which follows LOGICALLY from the above passage is that

    A. burglar alarms employ sensor devices; robbery alarms make use of initiation devices
    B. robbery alarms signal intrusion without the help of the victim; burglar alarms require the victim to trigger a switch
    C. robbery alarms sound locally; burglar alarms are transmitted to a central agency
    D. the mechanisms for a burglar alarm and a robbery alarm are alike

49._____

50. According to the above passage, alarms can be located

    A. in a wide variety of settings
    B. only in enclosed areas
    C. at low cost in high-crime areas
    D. only in places where potential criminals will be deterred

50._____

51. According to the above passage, which of the following is ESSENTIAL if a signal is to be received in a central office?   51.___

    A. A foot or wall switch
    B. A noise producing mechanism
    C. A portable reception device
    D. Information regarding the location of the source

52. According to the above passage, an alarm system can function WITHOUT a   52.___

    A. centralized annunciating device
    B. device to stop the alarm
    C. sensing or initiating device
    D. transmission device

53. According to the above passage, the purpose of robbery alarms is to   53.___

    A. find out automatically whether a robbery has taken place
    B. lower the crime rate in high-crime areas
    C. make a loud noise to frighten away the criminal
    D. provide a victim with the means to signal for help

54. According to the above passage, alarms might aid in lessening crime if they were   54.___

    A. answered promptly by police
    B. completely automatic
    C. easily accessible to victims
    D. hidden and widespread

55. Of the following, the BEST title for the above passage is   55.___

    A. Detection of Crime by Alarms
    B. Lowering the Crime Rate
    C. Suppression of Crime
    D. The Prevention of Robbery

KEY (CORRECT ANSWERS)

1. C	11. C	21. D	31. D	41. A	51. D
2. C	12. D	22. B	32. B	42. B	52. A
3. B	13. A	23. C	33. A	43. B	53. D
4. B	14. D	24. A	34. C	44. B	54. D
5. B	15. A	25. B	35. C	45. C	55. A
6. D	16. A	26. C	36. D	46. D	
7. C	17. B	27. D	37. B	47. C	
8. B	18. B	28. A	38. A	48. A	
9. C	19. B	29. B	39. A	49. A	
10. D	20. B	30. D	40. D	50. A	

EXAMINATION SECTION
TEST 1

DIRECTIONS: Each question or incomplete statement is followed by several suggested answers or completions. Select the one that BEST answers the question or completes the statement. *PRINT THE LETTER OF THE CORRECT ANSWER IN THE SPACE AT THE RIGHT.*

1. As an administrative aide, it is your job to type reports prepared by several patrolmen. These reports are then returned to them for review and signature. Patrolman X consistently submits reports to you which contain misspellings and incorrect punctuation. Of the following, the BEST action for you to take is to

    A. tell your supervisor that something must be done about Patrolman X's poor English
    B. ask Patrolman X for permission to correct any mistakes
    C. assemble all of the patrolmen and tell them that you refuse to correct their mistakes
    D. tell Patrolman X to be more careful

1.____

2. On a chart used in your precinct, there appear small figures of men, women, and children to denote population trends. Your supervisor assigns you to suggest possible symbols for a chart which will be used to indicate daily vehicular traffic flow in the area covered by this precinct.
In this situation, your BEST course of action would be to

    A. tell your supervisor an artist should be hired to draw these symbols
    B. make up a list of possible symbols, such as cars and trucks
    C. say that any decision as to the symbols to be used should be made at a higher level
    D. find out how many vehicles use the area

2.____

3. As an administrative aide, you are assigned to the telephone switchboard. An extremely irate citizen calls complaining in bigoted terms about a group of Black teenagers who congregate in front of his house. The caller insists on speaking to whoever is in charge. At the moment, Sergeant X, a black man, is in charge.
The BEST course of action for you to take is to

    A. inform the caller that the teenagers may meet wherever they wish
    B. tell the caller that Sergeant X, a black man, is in charge, and ask him to call back later when a white man will be there
    C. tell the caller that you resent his bigotry and insist that he call back when he has calmed down
    D. acquaint Sergeant X with the circumstances and connect the caller with him

3.____

4. Assume that you have access to restricted materials such as conviction records. A friend asks you, unofficially, if a man he has recently met has a record of conviction.
The BEST thing for you to do is to

    A. give your friend the information he wants and inform your supervisor of your actions
    B. tell your friend that you are not allowed to give out such information
    C. tell your friend you will try to get the information for him but do not take any action
    D. give him the information because it is a matter of public record

4.____

5. Assume that you are an administrative aide assigned to a busy telephone information center.
    Of the following, which is the MOST important technique to use when answering the telephone?

    A. Using many technical police terms
    B. Speaking slowly, in a monotone, for clarity
    C. Using formal English grammar
    D. Speaking clearly and distinctly

5.__

6. As an administrative aide, you are asked by an officer working in an adjacent office to type a very important letter without mistakes or corrections exactly as he has prepared it. As you are typing, you notice a word which, according to the dictionary, is misspelled. Under the circumstances, you should

    A. ignore the error and type it exactly as prepared
    B. change the spelling without telling the officer
    C. ask the officer if you should change the spelling
    D. change the spelling and tell the officer

6.__

7. As an administrative aide, you are in charge of a large complex of files. In an effort to be helpful, some officers who frequently use the file have begun to refile material they had been using. Unfortunately, they often make errors.
    Of the following, your BEST course of action is to

    A. ask them to leave the files for you to put away
    B. ask your supervisor to reprimand them
    C. frequently check the whole filing system for errors
    D. tell them they are making mistakes and insist they leave the files alone

7.__

8. One afternoon several of the police officers ask you to do different tasks. Each task will take about half a day to complete, but each officer insists that his work must be completed immediately.
    Your BEST course of action is to

    A. do a little of each assignment given to you
    B. ask your fellow workers to help you with the assignment
    C. speak to your supervisor in order to determine the priority of the assignments
    D. do the work in the order of the rank of the officers giving the assignments

8.__

Questions 9-12.

DIRECTIONS: Questions 9 through 12 are to be answered on the basis of the following passage.

It should be emphasized that one goal of law enforcement is the reduction of stress between one population group and another. When no stress exists between populations, law enforcement can deal with other tensions or simply perform traditional police functions. However, when stress between populations does exist, law enforcement, in its efforts to prevent disruptive behavior, becomes committed to reducing that stress (if for no other reason than its responsibility to maintain an orderly environment). The type of stress to be reduced, unlike the tension stemming from social change, is stress generated through intergroup and interracial friction. Of course, all sources of tension are inextricably interrelated, but friction between different populations in the community is of immediate concern to law enforcement.

9. The above passage emphasizes that, during times of stress between groups in the community, it is necessary for the police to attempt to

    A. continue their traditional duties
    B. eliminate tension resulting from social change
    C. reduce intergroup stress
    D. punish disruptive behavior.

9.____

10. Based on the above passage, police concern with tension among groups in a community is MOST likely to stem prinarily from their desire to

    A. establish racial justice   B. prevent violence
    C. protect property   D. unite the diverse groups

10.____

11. According to the above passage, enforcers of the law are responsible for

    A. analyzing consequences of population-group hostility
    B. assisting social work activities
    C. creating order in the environment
    D. explaining group behavior

11.____

12. The factor which produces the tension accompanying social change is

    A. a disorderly environment
    B. disruptive behavior
    C. inter-community'hostility
    D. not discussed in the above passage

12.____

Questions 13-19.

DIRECTIONS: Questions 13 through 19 are to be answered on the basis of the information given in the passage below.

From a nationwide point of view, the need for new housing units during the years immediately ahead will be determined by four major factors. The most important factor is the net change in household formations -- that is, the difference between the number of new households that are formed and the number of existing households that are dissolved, whether by death or other circumstances. During the 1990's, as the children born during the decades of the 60's and 70's come of age and marry, the total number of households is expected to increase at a rate of more than 1,000,000 annually. The second factor affecting the need for new housing units is *removals* -- that is, existing units that are demolished, damaged beyond repair, or otherwise removed from the housing supply. A third factor is the number of existing vacancies. To some extent, vacancies can satisfy the housing demand caused by increases in total number of households or by removals, although population shifts that are already under way mean that some areas will have a surfeit of vacancies and other areas will be faced with serious shortages of housing. A final factor, and one that has only recently assumed major importance, is the increasing demand for second homes. These may take any form from a shack in the woods for the city dweller to a *pied-a-terre* in the city for a suburbanite. Whatever the form, however, it is certain that increasing leisure time, rising amounts of discretionary income, and improvements in transportation are leading more and more Americans to look on a second home not as a rich man's luxury but as the common man's right.

13. The above passage uses the term *housing units* to refer to   13.__

    A. residences of all kinds
    B. apartment buildings only
    C. one-family houses only
    D. the total number of families in the United States

14. The passage uses the word *removals* to mean   14.__

    A. the shift of population from one area to another
    B. vacancies that occur when families move
    C. financial losses suffered when a building is damaged or destroyed
    D. former dwellings that are demolished or can no longer be used for housing

15. The expression *pied-a-terre* appears in the next-to-last sentence in the passage. A per-   15.__
son who is not familiar with the expression should be able to tell from the way it is used
here that it *probably* means

    A. a suburban home owned by a commuter
    B. a shack in the woods
    C. a second home that is used from time to time
    D. overnight lodging for a traveler in a strange city

16. Of the factors described in the passage as having an important influence on the demand   16.__
for housing, which factor-- taken alone -- is LEAST likely to encourage the construction
of new housing?
The

    A. net change in household formations
    B. destruction of existing housing
    C. existence of vacancies
    D. use of second homes

17. Based on the above passage, the TOTAL increase in the number of households during   17.__
the 1990's is expected to be MOST NEARLY

    A. 1,000,000   B. 10,000,000
    C. 100,000,000   D. 1,000,000,000

18. Which one of the following conclusions could MOST logically be drawn from the informa-   18.__
tion given in the passage?

    A. The population of the United States is increasing at the rate of about 1,000,000
       people annually.
    B. There is already a severe housing shortage in all parts of the country.
    C. The need for additional housing units is greater in some parts of the country than in
       others.
    D. It is still true that only wealthy people can afford to keep up more than one home.

19. Which one of the following conclusions could NOT logically be drawn from the informa- 19.____
tion given in the passage?

    A.   The need for new housing will be even greater in the 2000's than in the 1990's.
    B.   Demolition of existing housing must be taken into account in calculating the need
        for new housing construction.
    C.   Having a second home is more common today than it was in the 1960's.
    D.   Part of the housing needs of the 1990's can be met by vacancies.

20. You are making a report on the number of incoming calls handled by two different switch- 20.____
boards. Over a five-day period, the total count of incoming calls per day for both switch-
boards together was 2,773. The average number of incoming calls per day for
Switchboard A was 301.
You cannot find one day's tally for Switchboard B, but the total for the other four days
for Switchboard B comes to 1,032.
Determine from this how many incoming calls must have been reported on the *missing*
tally for Switchboard B.

    A.   236   B.   258   C.   408   D.   1,440

21. Assume that one-page notices for distribution may be reproduced by photocopy or by 21.____
stencil. The cost for photocopying is 5 1/2 cents per copy. It can also be reproduced by
the stencil method for an initial preparation cost of $1.38 plus a per-copy cost of one
cent. Strictly according to cost, which of the following is the LOWEST number of copies
at which it would be more economical to choose the stencil method instead of photocopying?

    A.   15   B.   30   C.   45   D.   138

22. An employee completed 75% of a clerical assignment in four days. How much of it did he 22.____
complete in the last two days if he finished 3/8 of it in the first two days?

    A.   1/4   B.   3/8   C.   5/8   D.   3/4

23. Seven hundred people are to be scheduled for interviews. If 58% of these 700 people 23.____
have already been scheduled, how many more must be scheduled?

    A.   138   B.   294   C.   406   D.   410

24. In recent years, an average of 35% of the violations reported in any given month have 24.____
been corrected by the time of a follow-up inspection one month later. Last month, 240
violations were reported, and this month's follow-up inspections show that 93 of them
have been corrected.
How many more violations have been corrected than would have been expected,
based on the average rate?

    A.   5   B.   9   C.   33   D.   58

25. Suppose that, on a scaled drawing of an office floor plan, 1/2 inch equals 2 feet. 25.____
An office that is actually 12 feet wide and 17 feet long has which of the following
dimensions on this scaled drawing?
_____ wide and _____ long.

    A.   3"; 4.25"   B.   6"; 8.5"   C.   12"; 17"   D.   24"; 34"

KEY (CORRECT ANSWERS)

1.	B		11.	C
2.	B		12.	D
3.	D		13.	A
4.	B		14.	D
5.	D		15.	C
6.	C		16.	C
7.	A		17.	B
8.	C		18.	C
9.	C		19.	A
10.	B		20.	A

21. C
22. B
23. B
24. B
25. A

————————

TEST 2

DIRECTIONS: Each question or incomplete statement is followed by several suggested
answers or completions. Select the one that BEST answers the question or
completes the statement. *PRINT THE LETTER OF THE CORRECT ANSWER
IN THE SPACE AT THE RIGHT.*

1. Suppose that employees in a certain division put in a total of 1,250 hours of overtime in   1._____
1999. In 2000, total overtime hours for the same division were 2% less than in 1999, but
in 2001 overtime hours increased by 8% over the 2000 total.
How many overtime hours were worked by the staff of this division in 2001?

    A. 1,323   B. 1,331   C. 1,350   D. 1,375

2. A particular operation currently involves 75 employees, 80% of whom work in the field   2._____
and the rest of whom are office staff. A management study has shown that in order to be
truly efficient, the operation should have a ratio of at least 1 office employee to every 3
field employees, and the study recommends that the number of field employees remain
the same as at present.
What is the MINIMUM number of employees needed to carry out the operation efficiently, according to this recommendation?

    A. 65   B. 75   C. 80   D. 100

Questions 3-6.

DIRECTIONS: Questions 3 through 6 are to be answered on the basis of the information
given in the passage below.

Data processing is by no means a new invention. In one form or another, it has been carried on throughout the entire history of civilization. In its most general sense, data processing
means organizing data so that it can be used for a specific purpose a procedure commonly
known simply as *record-keeping* or *paperwork.* With the development of modern office equipment, and particularly with the recent introduction of computers, the techniques of data processing have become highly elaborate and sophisticated, but the basic purpose remains the
same: turning raw data into useful information.

The key concept here is usefulness. The data, or input, that is to be processed can be
compared to the raw material that is to go into a manufacturing process. The information, or
output, that results from data processing -- like the finished product of a manufacturer --
should be clearly usable. A collection of data has little value unless it is converted into information that serves a specific function.

3. The expression *paperwork,* as it is used in this passage,   3._____

    A.   shows that the author regards such operations as a waste of time
    B.   has the same general meaning as *data processing*
    C.   refers to methods of record-keeping that are no longer in use
    D.   indicates that the public does not understand the purpose of data processing

4. The passage indicates that the use of computers has

    A. greatly simplified the clerical work in an office
    B. led to more complicated systems for the handling of data
    C. had no effect whatsoever on data processing
    D. made other modern office machines obsolete

4.__

5. Which of the following BEST expresses the basic principle of data processing as it is described in the passage?

    A. Input - processing - output
    B. Historical record-keeping - modern techniques - specific functions
    C. Office equipment - computer - accurate data
    D. Raw material - manufacturer - retailer

5.__

6. According to the above passage, data processing may be described as

    A. a new management technique
    B. computer technology
    C. information output
    D. record-keeping

6.__

Questions 7-10.

DIRECTIONS: Questions 7 through 10 are to be answered on the basis of the following passage.

Analysis of current data reveals that motor vehicle transportation actually requires less space than was used for other types of transportation in the pre-automobile era, even including the substantial area taken by freeways. The reason is that when the fast-moving through traffic is put on built-for-the-purpose arterial roads, then the amount of ordinary space needed for strictly local movement and for access to property drops sharply. Even the amount of land taken for urban expressways turns out to be surprisingly small in terms either of total urban acreage or of the volume of traffic they carry. No existing or contemplated urban expressway system requires as much as 3 percent of the land in the areas it serves, and this would be exceptionally high. The Los Angeles freeway system, when complete, will occupy only 2 percent of the available land; the same is true of the District of Columbia, where only 0.75 percent will be pavement, with the remaining 1.25 percent as open space. California studies estimate that, in a typical California urban community, 1.6 to 2 percent of the area should be devoted to freeways, which will handle 50 to 60 percent of all traffic needs, and about ten times as much land to the ordinary roads and streets that carry the rest of the traffic. By comparison, when John A. Sutter laid out Sacramento in 1850, he provided 38 percent of the area for streets and sidewalks. The French architect, Pierre L'Enfant, proposed 59 percent of the area of the District of Columbia for roads and streets; urban renewal in Southwest Washington, incorporating a modern street network, reduced the acreage of space for pedestrian and vehicular traffic in the renewal area from 48.2 to 41.5 percent of the total. If we are to have a reasonable consideration of the impact of highway transportation on contemporary urban development, it would be well to understand these relationships.

7. The author of this passage says that 　　　　　　　　　　　　　　　　　　　　　　　7.＿＿

    A. modern transportation uses less space than was used for transportation before the auto age
    B. expressways require more space than streets in terms of urban acreage
    C. typical urban communities were poorly designed in terms of relationship between space used for traffic and that used for other purposes
    D. the need for local and access roads would increase if the number of expressways were increased

8. According to the above passage, it was originally planned that the percent of the area to 　　8.＿＿
be used for roads and streets in the District of Columbia should be MOST NEARLY

    A. 40%   B. *45%*   C. 50%   D. 60%

9. The above passage states that the amount of space needed for local traffic 　　　　　　　9.＿＿

    A. *increases* when arterial highways are constructed
    B. *decreases* when arterial highways are constructed
    C. *decreases* when there is more land available
    D. *increases* when there is more land available

10. According to the above passage, studies estimate that, in a typical California urban com- 　10.＿＿
munity, the amount of land devoted to ordinary roads and streets as compared with that devoted to freeways should be MOST NEARLY ＿＿＿＿ as much.

    A. one-half   B. one-tenth   C. twice   D. ten times

Questions 11-13.

DIRECTIONS: Questions 11 through 13 are to be answered on the basis of the following passage.

A glaring exception to the usual practice of the judicial trial as a means of conflict resolution is the utilization of administrative hearings. The growing tendency to create administrative bodies with rule-making and quasi-judicial powers has shattered many standard concepts. A comprehensive examination of the legal process cannot neglect these newer patterns.

In the administrative process, the legislative, executive, and judicial functions are mixed together, and many functions, such as investigating, advocating, negotiating, testifying, rule-making, and adjudicating, are carried out by the same agency. The reason for the breakdown of the separation-of-powers formula is not hard to find. It was felt by Congress, and state and municipal legislatures, that certain regulatory tasks could not be performed efficiently, rapidly, expertly, and with due concern for the public interest by the traditional branches of government. Accordingly, regulatory agencies were delegated powers to consider disputes from the earliest stage of investigation to the final stages of adjudication entirely within each agency itself, subject only to limited review in the regular courts.

11. The above passage states that the usual means for conflict resolution is through the use 　11.＿＿
of

    A. judicial trial   B. administrative hearing
    C. legislation   D. regulatory agencies

12. The above passage *implies* that the use of administrative hearing in resolving conflict is   12.___
a(n) _____ approach.

    A. traditional   B. new
    C. dangerous   D. experimental

13. The above passage states that the reason for the breakdown of the separation-of-powers   13.___
formula in the administrative process is that

    A. Congress believed that certain regulatory tasks could be better performed by separate agencies
    B. legislative and executive functions are incompatible in the same agency
    C. investigative and regulatory functions are not normally reviewed by the courts
    D. state and municipal legislatures are more concerned with efficiency than with legality

14. An employee examining the summonses of individuals appearing for hearings noticed   14.___
that the address one one summons was the same as that of an individual who had
appeared earlier that day. He asked the second respondent if he knew the first respondent.
The MOST appropriate evaluation of the employee's behavior is that he should

    A. not have mentioned any other respondent to the second respondent
    B. not waste time inspecting summonses in such detail
    C. be commended for inspecting summonses so carefully
    D. be commended for his investigation of the respondents

15. An employee is assigned to maintain all types of frequently used reference materials   15.___
such as booklets and technical papers. He keeps these in a pile on a shelf in order of
arrival. When new material arrives, he puts it on top of the pile. Which of the following
BEST evaluates the employee's handling of this reference material? His system is MOST
likely to result in _____ filing and _____ retrieval.

    A. fast; slow   B. slow; slow
    C. fast; fast   D. slow; fast

16. An employee computes statistics relating to proceedings. The method he devised con-   16.___
sists of organizing his source . and summary documents in such a manner that at any
time another employee can assume the work. This method takes a little more time than
other possible methods.
Which of the following statements BEST evaluates the judgment of the employee in
devising such a method?
The employee has used

    A. *good* judgment because it is important to provide for continuity
    B. *poor* judgment because he is not using the fastest method
    C. *good* judgment because, if a job is done as fast as possible, it becomes tiring
    D. *poor* judgment because it is not an employee's responsibility to prepare for a replacement

17. Assume that it is your job to receive incoming telephone calls. Those calls which you   17.___
cannot handle yourself have to be transferred to the appropriate office.
If you receive an outside call for an extension line which is busy, the one of the following which you should do FIRST is to

A. interrupt the person speaking on the extension and tell him a call is waiting
B. tell the caller the line is busy and let him know every thirty seconds whether or not it is free
C. leave the caller on *hold* until the extension is free
D. tell the caller the line is busy and ask him if he wishes to wait

18. On one occasion in a certain office, an elderly employee collapsed, apparently the victim of a heart attack. Chaos broke out in the office as several people tried to help him and several others tried to get assistance.
Of the following, the MOST certain way of avoiding such chaos in the future is to

18.____

A. keep a copy of heart attack procedures on file so that it can be referred to by any member of the staff when an emergency occurs
B. provide each member of the staff with a first aid book which is to be kept in an accessible location
C. train all members of the staff in the proper procedure for handling such emergencies, assigning specific responsibilities
D. post, in several places around the office, a list of specific procedures to follow in each of several different emergencies

19. Your superior has subscribed to several publications directly related to your division's work, and he has asked you to see to it that the publications are circulated among the supervisory personnel in the division. There are eight supervisors involved.
The BEST method of insuring that all eight see these publications is to

19.____

A. place the publication in the division's general reference library as soon as it arrives
B. inform each supervisor whenever a publication arrives and remind all of them that they are responsible for reading it
C. prepare a standard slip that can be stapled to each publication, listing the eight supervisors and saying, *Please read, initial your name, and pass along*
D. send a memo to the eight supervisors saying that they may wish to purchase individual subscriptions in their own names if they are interested in seeing each issue

20. Assume that you have been asked to prepare a narrative summary of the monthly reports submitted by employees in your division.
In preparing your summary of this month's reports, the FIRST step to take is to

20.____

A. read through the reports, noting their general content and any unusual features
B. decide how many typewritten pages your summary should contain
C. make a written summary of each separate report, so that you will not have to go back to the original reports again
D. ask each employee which points he would prefer to see emphasized in your summary

21. Your superior has telephoned a number of key officials in your agency to ask whether they can meet at a certain time next month. He has found that they can all make it, and he has asked you to confirm the meeting.
Which of the following is the BEST way to confirm such a meeting?

21.____

A. Note the meeting on your superior's calendar
B. Post a notice of the meeting on the agency bulletin board
C. Call the officials on the day of the meeting to remind them of the meeting
D. Write a memo to each official involved repeating the time and place of the meeting

22. Of the following, the worker who is MOST likely to create a problem in maintaining safety is one who   22.___

    A. disregards hazards   B. feels tired
    C. resents authority   D. gets bored

23. Assume that a new regulation requires that certain kinds of private organizations file information forms with your department. You have been asked to write the short explanatory message that will be printed on the front cover of the pamphlet containing the forms and instructions. Which of the following would be the MOST appropriate way of beginning this message?   23.___

    A. Get the readers' attention by emphasizing immediately that there are legal penalties for organizations that fail to file before a certain date
    B. Briefly state the nature of the enclosed forms and the types of organizations that must file
    C. Say that your department is very sorry to have to put organizations to such an inconvenience
    D. Quote the entire regulation adopted by the city, even if it is quite long and is expressed in complicated legal language

24. Suppose that you have been told to make up the vacation schedule for the 15 employees in a particular unit. In order for the unit to operate effectively, only a few employees can be on vacation at the same time.
Which of the following is the MOST advisable approach in making up the schedule?   24.___

    A. Draw up a schedule assigning vacations in alphabetical order
    B. Find out when the supervisors want to take their vacations, and randomly assign whatever periods are left to the non-supervisory personnel
    C. Assign the most desirable times to employees of longest standing, and the least desirable times to the newest employees
    D. Have all employees state their own preferences, and then work out any conflicts in consultation with the people involved

25. Assume that you have been asked to prepare job descriptions for various positions in your department.
Which of the following are the BASIC points that should be covered in a job description?   25.___

    A. General duties and responsibilities of the position, with examples of day-to-day tasks
    B. Comments on the performances of present employees
    C. Estimates of the number of openings that may be available in each category during the coming year
    D. Instructions for carrying out the specific tasks assigned to your department

KEY (CORRECT ANSWERS)

1.	A		11.	A
2.	C		12.	B
3.	B		13.	A
4.	B		14.	A
5.	A		15.	A
6.	D		16.	A
7.	A		17.	D
8.	D		18.	C
9.	B		19.	C
10.	D		20.	A

21.	D
22.	A
23.	B
24.	D
25.	A

_____

TEST 3

DIRECTIONS: Each question or incomplete statement is followed by several suggested answers or completions. Select the one that BEST answers the question or completes the statement. *PRINT THE LETTER OF THE CORRECT ANSWER IN THE SPACE AT THE RIGHT.*

Questions 1-6.

DIRECTIONS: Questions 1 through 6 consist of sets of names and addresses. In each question, the name and address in Column II should be an exact copy of the name and address in Column I. If there is:

    a mistake only in the name, mark your answer A,
    a mistake only in the address, mark your answer B,
    a mistake in both name and address, mark your answer C,
    NO mistake in either name or address, mark your answer D.

SAMPLE QUESTION

COLUMN I	COLUMN II
Christina Magnusson	Christina Magnusson
288 Greene Street	288 Greene Street
New York, NY 10013	New York, NY 10003

Since there is a mistake only in the address (the zone number should be 10003 instead of 10013), the answer to the sample question is B.

	COLUMN I	COLUMN II	
1.	Ms. Joan Kelly 313 Franklin Ave. Brooklyn, NY 11202	Ms. Joan Kielly 318 Franklin Ave. Brooklyn, NY 11202	1.__
2.	Mrs. Eileen Engel 47-24 86 Road Queens, NY 11122	Mrs. Ellen Engel 47-24 86 Road Queens, NY 11122	2.__
3.	Marcia Michaels 213 E. 81 St. New York, NY 10012	Marcia Michaels 213 E. 81 St. New York, NY 10012	3.__
4.	Rev. Edward J. Smyth 1401 Brandeis Street San Francisco, CA 96201	Rev. Edward J. Smyth 1401 Brandies Street San Francisco, CA 96201	4.__
5.	Alicia Rodriguez 24-68 81 St. Elmhurst, NY 11122	Alicia Rodriguez 2468 81 St. Elmhurst, NY 11122	5.__
6.	Ernest Eisemann 21 Columbia St. New York, NY 10007	Ernest Eisermann 21 Columbia St. New York, NY 10007	6.__

Questions 7-11.

DIRECTIONS: Questions 7 through 11 each consist of five serial numbers which must be arranged according to the directions given below.

The serial numbers of dollar bills in Column I begin and end with a capital letter and have an eight-digit number in between. They are to be arranged as follows:

First: In alphabetical order according to the first letter
Second: When two or more serial numbers have the same first letter, in alphabetical order according to the last letter
Third: When two or more serial numbers have the same first and last letters, in numerical order, beginning with the lowest number

The serial numbers in Column I are numbered 1 through 5 in the order in which they are listed. In Column II, the numbers 1 through 5 are arranged in four different ways to show different arrangements of the corresponding serial numbers. Choose the answer in Column II in which the serial numbers are arranged according to the above rules.

SAMPLE QUESTION

COLUMN I	COLUMN II
1. E75044127B	A. 4, 1, 3, 2, 5
2. B96399104A	B. 4, 1, 2, 3, 5
3. B93939086A	C. 4, 3, 2, 5, 1
4. B47064465H	D. 3, 2, 5, 4, 1
5. B99040922A	

In the sample question, the four serial numbers starting with B should be put before the serial number starting with E. The serial numbers starting with B and ending with A should be put before the serial number starting with B and ending with H. The three serial numbers starting with B and ending with A should be listed in numerical order, beginning with the lowest number. The correct way to arrange the serial numbers, therefore, is:

3.	B93939086A
2.	B96399104A
5.	B99040922A
4.	B47064465H
1.	E75044127B

Since the order of arrangement is 3, 2, 5, 4, 1, the answer to the sample question is D.

	COLUMN I		COLUMN II	
7.				7.___
	1. S55126179E	A.	1, 5, 2, 3,4	
	2. R55136177Q	B.	3, 4, 1, 5, 2	
	3. P55126177R	C.	3, 5, 2, 1, 4	
	4. S55126178R	D.	4, 3, 1, 5, 2	
	5. R55126180P			

8.				8.___
	1. T64217813Q	A.	4, 1, 3, 2, 5	
	2. I64217817O	B.	2, 4, 3, 1, 5	
	3. T64217818O	C.	4, 1, 5, 2, 3	
	4. I64217811Q	D.	2, 3, 4, 1, 5	
	5. T64217816Q			

9.				9.___
	1. C83261824G	A.	2, 4, 1, 5,3	
	2. C78361833C	B.	4, 2, 1, 3, 5	
	3. G83261732G	C.	3, 1, 5, 2, 4	
	4. C88261823C	D.	2, 3, 5, 1, 4	
	5. G83261743C			

10.				10.___
	1. A11710107H	A.	2, 1, 4, 3, 5	
	2. H17110017A	B.	3, 1, 5, 2, 4	
	3. A11170707A	C.	3, 4, 1, 5, 2	
	4. II17170171H	D.	3, 5, 1, 2, 4	
	5. A11710177A			

11.				11.___
	1. R26794821S	A.	3, 2,4, 1, 5	
	2. O26794821T	B.	3, 4, 2, 1, 5	
	3. M26794827Z	C.	4, 2, 1, 3, 5	
	4. Q26794821R	D.	5, 4, 1, 2, 3	
	5. S26794821P			

Questions 12-16.

DIRECTIONS: Questions 12 through 16 each consist of three lines of code letters and numbers. The numbers on each line should correspond with the code letters on the same line in accordance with the table below.

Code Letters	Q	S	L	Y	M	O	U	N	W	Z
Corresponding Numbers	1	2	3	4	5	6	7	8	9	0

On some of the lines, an error exists in the coding. Compare the letters and numbers in each question carefully. If you find an error on:

only ONE of the lines in the question, mark your answer A,
any TWO lines in the question, mark your answer B,
all THREE lines in the question, mark your answer C,
NONE of the lines in the question, mark your answer D.

SAMPLE:

MOQNWZQS - 56189012
QWNMOLYU - 19865347
LONLMYWN - 36835489

In the above sample, the first line is correct since each code letter, as listed, has the correct corresponding number. On the second line, an error exists because code letter M should have the nuriber 5 instead of the number 6. On the third line, an error exists - because the code letter W should have the number 9 instead of the nuriber 8. Since there are errors on two of the three lines, the correct answer is B.

12.	SMUWOLQN	25796318	12.____
	ULSQNMZL	73218503	
	NMYQZUSL	85410723	

13.	YUWWMYQZ	47995410	13.____
	SOSOSQSO	26262126	
	ZUNLWMYW	07839549	

14.	QULSWZYN	17329045	14.____
	ZYLQWOYW	04319639	
	QLUYWZSO	13749026	

15.	NLQZOYUM	83106475	15.____
	SQMUWZOM	21579065	
	MMYWMZSQ	55498021	

16.	NQLOWZZU	81319007	16.____
	SMYLUNZO	25347806	
	UWMSNZOL	79528013	

Questions 17-24.

DIRECTIONS: Each of Questions 17 through 24 represents five cards to be filed, numbered 1 through 5 in Column I. Each card is made up of the employee's name, the date of a work assignment, and the work assignment code number shown in parentheses. The cards are to be filed according to the following rules:

First: File in alphabetical order
Second: When two or more cards have the same employee's name, file according to the assignment date beginning with the earliest date
Third: When two or more cards have the same employee's name and the same date, file according to the work assignment number beginning with the lowest number.

Column II shows the cards arranged in four different orders. Pick the answer (A, B, C, or D) in Column II which shows the cards arranged correctly according to the above filing rules.

SAMPLE QUESTION

	COLUMN I				COLUMN II
1.	Cluney	4/8/72	(486503)	A.	2, 3, 4, 1, 5
2.	Roster	5/10/7	(246611)	B.	2, 5, 1, 3, 4
3.	Altool	10/15/72	(711433)	C.	3, 2, 1, 4, 5
4.	Cluney	2/18/72	(527610)	D.	3, 5, 1, 4, 2
5.	Cluney	4/8/72	(486500)		

The correct way to file the cards is:

3.	Altool	10/15/72	(711433)
5.	Cluney	4/8/72	(486500)
1.	Cluney	4/8/72	(486503)
4.	Cluney	12/18/72	(527610)
2.	Roster	5/10/71	(246611)

The correct filing order is shown by the numbers in front of each name (3, 5, 1, 4, 2). The answer to the sample question is the letter in Column II in front of the numbers 3, 5, 1, 4, 2. This answer is D.

Now answer Questions 17 through 24 according to these rules.

17.

	COLUMN I				COLUMN II
1.	Kohls	4/2/72	(125677)	A.	1, 2, 3, 4, 5
2.	Keller	3/21/72	(129698)	B.	3, 2, 1, 4, 5
3.	Jackson	4/10/72	(213541)	C.	3, 1, 2, 4, 5
4.	Richards	1/9/73	(347236)	D.	5, 2, 1, 3, 4
5.	Richmond	12/11/71	(379321)		

17.___

18.

1.	Burroughs	5/27/72	(237896)	A.	1, 4, 3, 2, 5
2.	Charlson	1/16/72	(114537)	B.	4, 1, 5, 3, 2
3.	Carlsen	12/2/72	(114377)	C.	1, 4, 3, 5, 2
4.	Burton	5/1/72	(227096)	D.	4, 1, 3, 5, 2
5.	Charlson	12/2/72	(114357)		

18.___

19.

1.	Ungerer	11/11/72	(537924)	A.	1, 5, 3, 2, 4
2.	Winters	11/10/72	(657834)	B.	5, 1, 3, 4, 2
3.	Ventura	12/1/72	(698694)	C.	3, 5, 1, 2, 4
4.	winters	10/11/72	(675654)	D.	1, 5, 3, 4, 2
5.	Ungaro	11/10/72	(684325)		

19.___

20.

1.	Norton	3/12/73	(071605)	A.	1, 4, 2, 4, 5
2.	Morris	2/26/73	(068931)	B.	3, 5, 2, 4, 1
3.	Morse	5/12/73	(142358)	C.	2, 4, 3, 5, 1
4.	Morris	2/26/73	(068391)	D.	4, 2, 5, 3, 1
5.	Morse	2/26/73	(068391)		

20.___

21.

1.	Eger	4/19/72	(874129)	A.	3, 4, 1, 2, 5
2.	Eihler	5/19/73	(875329)	B.	1, 4, 5, 2, 3
3.	Ehrlich	11/19/72	(874839)	C.	4, 1, 3, 2, 5
4.	Eger	4/19/72	(876129)	D.	1, 4, 3, 5, 2
5.	Eihler	5/19/72	(874239)		

21.___

	COLUMN I				COLUMN II	

22.
1.	Johnson	12/21/72	(786814)
2.	Johns	12/21/73	(801024)
3.	Johnson	12/12/73	(762814)
4.	Jackson	12/12/73	(862934)
5.	Johnson	12/12/73	(762184)

A. 2, 4, 3, 5, 1
B. 4, 2, 5, 3, 1
C. 4, 5, 3, 1, 2
D. 5, 3, 1, 2, 4

22.____

23.
1.	Fuller	7/12/72	(598310)
2.	Fuller	7/2/72	(598301)
3.	Fuller	7/22/72	(598410)
4.	Fuller	7/17/73	(598710)
5.	Fuller	7/17/73	(598701)

A. 2, 1, 5, 4, 3
B. 1, 2, 4, 5, 3
C. 1, 4, 5, 2, 3
D. 2, 1, 3, 5, 4

23.____

24.
1.	Perrine	10/27/69	(637096)
2.	Perrone	11/14/72	(767609)
3.	Perrault	10/15/68	(629706)
4.	Perrine	10/17/72	(373656)
5.	Perine	10/17/71	(376356)

A. 3, 4, 5, 1, 2
B. 3, 2, 5, 4, 1
C. 5, 3, 1, 4, 2
D. 4, 5, 1, 2, 3

24.____

Questions 25-30.

DIRECTIONS: Questions 25 through 30 are to be answered on the basis of the information given in the passage below.

It is often said that no system will work if the people who carry it out do not want it to work. In too many cases, a departmental reorganization that seemed technically sound and economically practical has proved to be a failure because the planners neglected to take the human factor into account. The truth is that employees are likely to feel threatened when they learn that a major change is in the wind. It does not matter whether or not the change actually poses a threat to an employee; the fact that he believes it does or fears it might is enough to make him feel insecure. Among the dangers he fears, the foremost is the possibility that his job may cease to exist and that he may be laid off or shunted into a less skilled position at lower pay. Even if he knows that his own job category is secure, however, he is likely to fear losing some of the important intangible advantages of his present position for instance, he may fear that he will be separated from his present companions and thrust in with a group of strangers, or that he will find himself in a lower position on the organizational ladder if a new position is created above his.

It is important that management recognize these natural fears and take them into account in planning any kind of major change. While there is no cut-and-dried formula for pre-venting employee resistance, there are several steps that can be taken to reduce employees' fears and gain their cooperation. First, unwarranted fears can be dispelled if employees are kept informed of the planning from the start and if they know exactly what to expect. Next, assurance on matters such as retraining, transfers, and placement help should be given as soon as it is clear what direction the reorganization will take. Finally, employees' participation in the planning should be actively sought. There is a great psychological difference between feeling that a change is being forced upon one from the outside, and feeling that one is an insider who is helping to bring about a change.

25. According to the above passage, employees who are not in real danger of losing their   25.___
jobs because of a proposed reorganization

   A. will be eager to assist in the reorganization
   B. will pay little attention to the reorganization
   C. should not be taken into account in planning the reorganization
   D. are nonetheless likely to feel threatened by the reorganization.

26. The passage mentions the *intangible advantages* of a position. Which of the following   26.___
BEST describes the kind of advantages alluded to in the passage?

   A. Benefits such as paid holidays and vacations
   B. Satisfaction of human needs for things like friendship and status
   C. Qualities such as leadership and responsibility
   D. A work environment that meets satisfactory standards of health and safety

27. According to the passage, an employee's fear that a reorganization may separate him   27.___
from his present companions is a(n)

   A. childish and immature reaction to change
   B. unrealistic feeling, since this is not going to happen
   C. possible reaction that the planners should be aware of
   D. incentive to employees to participate in the planning

28. On the basis of the above passage, it would be *desirable,* when planning a departmental   28.___
reorganization, to

   A. be governed by employee feelings and attitudes
   B. give some employees lower positions
   C. keep employees informed
   D. lay off those who are less skilled

29. What does the passage say can be done to help gain employees' cooperation in a reor-   29.___
ganization?

   A. Making sure that the change is technically sound, that it is economically practical,
and that the human factor is taken into account
   B. Keeping employees fully informed, offering help in fitting them into new positions,
and seeking their participation in the planning
   C. Assuring employees that they will not be laid off, that they will not be reassigned to
a group of strangers, and that no new positions will be created on the organization
ladder
   D. Reducing employees' fears, arranging a retraining program, and providing for
transfers

30. Which of the following suggested titles would be MOST appropriate for this passage?   30.___

   A. PLANNING A DEPARTMENTAL REORGANIZATION
   B. WHY EMPLOYEES ARE AFRAID
   C. LOOKING AHEAD TO THE FUTURE
   D. PLANNING FOR CHANGE: THE HUMAN FACTOR

KEY (CORRECT ANSWERS)

1.	C	16.	C
2.	A	17.	B
3.	D	18.	A
4.	B	19.	B
5.	C	20.	D
6.	A	21.	D
7.	C	22.	B
8.	B	23.	D
9.	A	24.	C
10.	D	25.	D
11.	A	26.	B
12.	D	27.	C
13.	D	28.	C
14.	B	29.	B
15.	A	30.	D

EXAMINATION SECTION
TEST 1

DIRECTIONS: Each question or incomplete statement is followed by several suggested answers or completions. Select the one that BEST answers the question or completes the statement. *PRINT THE LETTER OF THE CORRECT ANSWER IN THE SPACE AT THE RIGHT.*

1. You answer a phone complaint from a person concerning an improper labeling practice in a shop in his neighborhood. Upon listening to the complaint, you get the impression that the person is exaggerating and may be too excited to view the matter clearly.
Of the following, your BEST course would be to

    A. tell the man that you can understand his anger but think it is not a really serious problem
    B. suggest to the man that he file a complaint with the Department of Consumer Affairs
    C. tell the man to stay away from the shop and have his friends do the same
    D. take down the information that the man offers so that he will see that the Police Department is concerned

1._____

2. Suppose that late at night you receive a call on 911.
The caller turns out to be an elderly man who is not able to get out much, and who is calling you not because he needs help but because he wants to talk with someone.
The BEST way to handle such a situation is to

    A. explain to him that the number is for emergencies and his call may prevent others from getting the help they need
    B. talk to him if not many calls are coming in but excuse yourself and cut him off if you are busy
    C. cut him off immediately when you find out he does not need help because this will be the most effective way of discouraging him
    D. suggest that he call train or bus information as the clerks there are often not busy at night

2._____

3. While you are on duty, you receive a call from a person whose name you recognize to be that of a person who calls frequently about matters of no importance. The caller requests your name and your supervisor's name so that she can report you for being impolite to her.
You should

    A. ask her when and how you were impolite to her
    B. tell her that she should not call about such minor matters
    C. make a report about her complaint for your superior
    D. give her the information that she requests

3._____

4. Of the following, the MOST important reason for requiring each employee of the Police Department to be responsible for good public relations is that

    A. the Police Department has better morale when employees join in an effort to improve public relations
    B. the public judges the Department according to impressions received at every level in the Department

4._____

C.   most employees will not behave well toward the public unless required to do so
D.   employees who improve public relations will receive commendations from superiors

5.   Assume that you are in the Bureau of Public Relations. You receive a telephone call from   5.__
     a citizen who asks if a study has been made of the advisability of combining the city's
     police and fire departments. Assume that you have no information on the subject.
     Of the following, your BEST course would be to

     A.   tell the caller that undoubtedly the subject has been studied, but that you do not
          have the information available
     B.   suggest to the caller that he telephone the Fire Department's Community Relations
          section for further information
     C.   explain to the caller that the functions of the two departments are distinct and that
          combining them would be inefficient
     D.   take the caller's number in order to call back, and then find information or referrals
          to give him

6.   Suppose that Police Department officials have discouraged representatives of the press   6.__
     from contacting police administrative aides (except aides in the Public Relations Bureau)
     for information.
     Of the following, the BEST reason for such a policy would be to

     A.   assure proper control over information released to the press by the Department
     B.   increase the value of official press releases of the Department
     C.   make press representatives realize that the Department is not seeking publicity
     D.   reduce the chance of crimes being committed in imitation of those reported in the
          press

7.   People who phone the Police Department often use excited, emotional, and sometimes   7.__
     angry speech.
     The BEST policy for you to take when speaking to this type of caller is to

     A.   tell the person directly that he must speak in a more civil way
     B.   tell the caller to call back when he is in a better mood
     C.   give the person time to settle down, by doing most of the talking yourself
     D.   speak calmly yourself to help the caller to gradually become more relaxed

8.   On a particularly busy evening, the police administrative aide assigned to the telephones   8.__
     had answered a tremendous number of inquiries and complaints by irate citizens.
     His patience was exhausted when he received a call from a citizen who reported,
     Officer, a bird just flew into my bedroom. What should I do? In a release of tension, the
     aide responded, *Keep it for seven days; and if no one claims it, it is yours.*
     This response by the aide would usually be considered

     A.   *advisable,* because the person should see how unusual his question was
     B.   *advisable,* because he avoided offering police services that were unavailable
     C.   *not advisable,* because such a remark might be regarded as insulting rather than
          humorous
     D.   *not advisable,* because the person might not want a bird for a pet

9. While temporarily assigned to switchboard duty, you receive a call from a man who says   9.____
his uncle in Pittsburgh has just called him and threatened to commit suicide. The man is
convinced his uncle intends to carry out his threat.
Of the following, you should

    A. advise the man to have neighbors of the uncle check to see if the uncle is all right
    B. politely inform the man that such out-of-town incidents are beyond the authority of
the local precinct
    C. take the uncle's name, address, and telephone number and immediately contact
police authorities in Pittsburgh
    D. get the man's name, address, and telephone number so that you can determine
whether the call is a hoax

10. Assume that in the course of your assigned duties, you have just taken a necessary   10.____
action which you feel has angered a citizen. After he has gone, you suddenly realize that
the incident might result in an unjustified complaint. The MOST advisable action for you
to take now would be to

    A. contact the person and apologize to him
    B. make complete notes on the incident and on any witnesses who might be helpful
    C. ask your superior what you might expect in case of such a complaint, without giv-
ing any hint of the actual occurrence
    D. accept the situation as one of the hazards of your job

11. Your job may bring you in contact with people from the community who are confronted   11.____
with emergencies, and are experiencing feelings of tension, anxiety, or even hostility. It is
good to keep in mind what attitude is most helpful to people who, in such situations, need
information and help. Suppose a person approaches you under circumstances like
these.
Which of the following would be BEST to do?

    A. Present similar examples of your own problems to make the person feel that his
problems are not unusual.
    B. Recognize the person's feelings, present information on available services, and
make suggestions as to proper procedures.
    C. Expect that some of the information is exaggerated and encourage the person to
let some time pass before seeking further help.
    D. Have the person wait while you try to make arrangements for his problem to be
solved.

12. Suppose that while on duty you receive a call from the owner of a gas station which is   12.____
located within the precinct. The owner is annoyed with a certain rule made by the Police
Department which concerns the operation of such stations. You agree with him.
Of the following, the BEST action for you to take is to

    A. make a report on the call and suggest to the owner that he write a letter to the
Department about the rule
    B. tell the owner that there is little that can be done since such rules are departmental
policy
    C. tell the owner that you agree with his complaint and that you will write a memo of
his call
    D. establish good relations with the owner by suggesting how to word a letter that will
get action from the Department

13. Suppose that you are working at the switchboard when a call comes in late at night from   13.___
a woman who reports that her neighbors are having a very noisy party. She gives you her
first name, surname, and address, and you ask whether her title is *Miss* or *Mrs.* She
replies that her title is irrelevant to her complaint, and wants to know why you ask.
Of the following possible ways of handling this, which is BEST?

    A. Insist that the title is necessary for identification purposes.
    B. Tell her that it is merely to find out what her marital status is.
    C. Agree that the information is not necessary and ask her how she wants to be
referred to.
    D. Find out why she shows such a peculiar reaction to a request for harmless informa-
tion.

14. While covering an assignment on the switchboard, you receive a call from a young girl   14.___
who tells you of rumored plans for a gang fight in her neighborhood.
You should

    A. take down the information so that a patrol squad can investigate the area and pos-
sibly keep the fight from starting
    B. discourage the girl from becoming alarmed by reminding her that it is only a rumor
    C. realize that this is a teenager looking for attention, humor her, and dismiss the mat-
ter
    D. take down the information but tell the girl that you need concrete information, and
not just rumors, to take any action on her call

15. The one of the following which would MOST likely lead to friction among police adminis-   15.___
trative aides in a unit would be for the supervisor in charge of the unit to

    A. defend the actions of the aides he supervises when discussing them with his own
supervisor
    B. get his men to work together as a team in completing the work of the unit
    C. praise each of the aides he supervises *in confidence* as the best aide in the unit
    D. consider the point of view of the aides he supervises when assigning unpleasant
tasks

16. Suppose that a police administrative aide who had been transferred to your office from   16.___
another unit in your Department because of difficulties with his supervisor has been
placed under your supervision.
The BEST course of action for you to take FIRST is to

    A. analyze the aide's past grievance to determine if the transfer was the best settle-
ment of the problem
    B. advise him of the difficulties his former supervisor had with other employees and
encourage him not to feel bad about the transfer
    C. warn him that you will not tolerate any nonsense and that he will be watched care-
fully while assigned to your unit
    D. instruct him in the duties he will be performing in your unit and make him feel
wanted in his new position

17. In which of the following circumstances would it be MOST appropriate for you to use an 17.____
impersonal style of writing rather than a personal style, which relies on the use of personal pronouns and other personal references?
When writing a memorandum to

    A. give your opinion to an associate on the advisability of holding a weekly staff meeting
    B. furnish your superior with data justifying a proposed outlay of funds for new equipment
    C. give your version of an incident which resulted in a complaint by a citizen about your behavior
    D. support your request for a transfer to another division

18. A newly appointed supervisor should learn as much as possible about the backgrounds 18.____
of his subordinates. The statement is generally CORRECT because

    A. effective handling of subordinates is based upon knowledge of their individual differences
    B. knowing their backgrounds assures they will be treated objectively, equally, and without favor
    C. some subordinates perform more efficiently under one supervisor than under another
    D. subordinates have confidence in a supervisor who knows all about them

19. You have found it necessary, for valid reasons, to criticize the work of one of the female 19.____
police administrative aides. She later comes to your desk and accuses you of criticizing her work because she is a woman.
The BEST way for you to deal with this employee is to

    A. ask her to apologize, since you would never allow yourself to be guilty of his kind of discrimination
    B. discuss her complaint with her, explaining again and at greater length the reason for your criticism
    C. assure her you wish to be fair, and ask her to submit a written report to you on her complaint
    D. apologize for hurting her feelings and promise that she will be left alone in the future

20. The following steps are recognized steps in teaching an employee a new skill: 20.____
    I. Demonstrate how to do the work
    II. Let the learner do the work himself
    III. Explain the nature and purpose of the work
    IV. Correct poor procedures by suggestion and demonstration
The CORRECT order for these steps is:

    A. III, II, IV, I   B. II, I, III, IV
    C. III, I, II, IV   D. I, III, II, IV

21. Suppose you have arranged an interview with a subordinate to try to help him overcome a serious shortcoming in his technical work. While you do not intend to talk to him about his attitude, you have noticed that he seems to be suspicious and resentful of people in authority. You need a record of the points covered in the discussion since further interviews are likely to be necessary.
Your BEST course would be to

    A. write a checklist of points you wish to discuss and carefully check the points off as the interview progresses
    B. know exactly how you wish to proceed, and then make written notes during the interview of your subordinate's comments
    C. frankly tell your subordinate that you are recording the talk on tape but place the recorder where it will not hinder discussion
    D. keep in mind what you wish to accomplish and make notes on the interview immediately after it is over

21.____

22. A police administrative aide has explained a complicated procedure to several subordinates. He has been talking clearly, allowing time for information to sink in. He has also encouraged questions. Yet, he still questions his subordinates after his explanation, with the obvious objective of finding out whether they completely understand the procedure. Under these circumstances, the action of the police administrative aide, in asking questions about the procedure, is

    A. *not advisable,* because subordinates who do not now know the procedure which has been explained so carefully can read and study it
    B. *not advisable,* because he endangers his relationship with his subordinates by insulting their intelligence
    C. *advisable,* because subordinates basically resent instructions and seldom give their full attention in a group situation
    D. *advisable,* because the answers to his questions help him to determine whether he has gained his objective

22.____

23. The most competent of the police administrative aides is a pleasant, intelligent young woman who breaks the rules of the Department by occasionally making long personal telephone calls during working hours. You have not talked to her up until now about this fault. However, the calls are beginning to increase, and you decide to deal directly with the problem.
The BEST way to approach the subject with her would be to

    A. review with her the history of her infractions of the rules
    B. point out that her conduct is not fair to the other workers
    C. tell her that her personal calls are excessive and discuss it with her
    D. warn her quietly that you intend to apply penalties if necessary

23.____

24. Assume that you are supervising eight male police administrative aides who do similar clerical work. A group of four of them work on each side of a row of files which can be moved without much trouble. You notice that in each group there is a clique of three aides, leaving one member isolated. The two isolated members are relative newcomers to the unit though they have been there a few months.
Your BEST course in such a case would be to

24.____

A. ignore the situation because to concern yourself with informal social arrangements of your subordinates would distract you from more important matters
B. ask each of the cliques to invite the isolated member in their working group to lunch with them from time to time
C. tell each group that you cannot allow cliques to form as it is bad for the morale of the unit
D. find an excuse to move the file cabinets to the side of the room and then move the desks of the two isolated members close together

25. Suppose that your supervisor, who has recently been promoted and transferred to your division, asks you to review a certain procedure with a view to its possible revision. You know that several years ago a sergeant made a lengthy and intensive report based on a similar review.
Which of the following would it be BEST for you to do FIRST?   25._____

A. Ask your supervisor if he is aware of the previous report.
B. Read the sergeant's report before you begin work to see what bearing it has on your assignment.
C. Begin work on the review without reading his report so that you will have a fresh point of view.
D. Ask the sergeant to assist you in your review.

26. Using form letters in business correspondence is LEAST effective when   26._____

A. answering letters on a frequently recurring subject
B. giving the same information to many addressees
C. the recipient is only interested in the routing information contained in the form letter
D. a reply must be keyed to the individual requirements of the intended reader

27. From the viewpoint of an office administrator, the BEST of the following reasons for distributing the incoming mail before the beginning of the regular work day is that   27._____

A. distribution can be handled quickly and most efficiently at that time
B. distribution later in the day may be distracting to or interfere with other employees
C. the employees who distribute the mail can then perform other tasks during the rest of the day
D. office activities for the day based on the mall may then be started promptly

28. Suppose you have had difficulty locating a document in the files because you could not decide where it should have been filed. You learn that other people in the office have had the same problem. You know that the document will be needed from time to time in the future.
Your BEST course, when refiling the document, would be to   28._____

A. make a written note of where you found it so that you will find it more easily the next time
B. reclassify it and file it in the file where you first looked for it
C. file it where you found it and put cross-reference sheets in the other likely files
D. make a mental association to help you find it the next time and put it back where you found it

29. Suppose that your supervisor is attending a series of meetings of police captains in Phil-   29.___
adelphia and will not be back until next Wednesday. He has left no instructions with you
as to how you should handle telephone calls for him.
In most instances, your BEST course would be to say,

    A. He isn't here just now
    B. He is out of town and won't be back until next Wednesday
    C. He won't be in today
    D. He is in Philadelphia attending a meeting of police captains

30. The one of the following which is USUALLY an important *by-product* of the preparation of   30.___
a procedure manual is that

    A. information uncovered in the process of preparation may lead to improvement of
       procedures
    B. workers refer to the manual instead of bothering their supervisors for information
    C. supervisors use the manual for training stenographers
    D. employees have equal access to information needed to do their jobs

31. You have been asked to organize a clerical job and supervise police administrative aides   31.___
who will do the actual work. The job consists of removing, from several boxes of data pro-
cessing cards which are arranged in alphabetical order, the cards of those whose names
appear on certain lists. The person removing the card then notes a date on the card.
Assume that the work will be done accurately whatever system is used.
Which of the following statements describes both the MOST efficient method and the
BEST reasons for using that method?
Have

    A. two aides work together, one calling names and the other extracting cards, and
       dating them, because the average production of any two aides working together
       should be higher, under these circumstances, than that of any two aides working
       alone
    B. each aide work alone, because it is easier to check spelling when reading the
       names than when listening to them
    C. two aides work together, one calling names and the other extracting cards and dat-
       ing them, because social interaction tends to make work go faster
    D. each aide work alone, because the average production of any two aides, each
       working alone, should be higher, under these circumstances, than that of any two
       aides working together

32. The term *work flow,* when used in connection with office management or the activities in   32.__
an office, generally means the

    A. rate of speed at which work flows through a single section of an office
    B. use of charts in the analysis of various office functions
    C. number of individual work units which can be produced by the average employee
    D. step-by-step physical routing of work through its various procedures

Questions 33-40.

DIRECTIONS:

Name of Offense	V A N D S B R U G H
Code Letter	c o m p l e x i t y
File Number	1 2 3 4 5 6 7 8 9 0

Assume that each of the above capital letters is the first letter of the name of an offense, that the small letter directly beneath each capital letter is the code letter for the offense, and that the number directly beneath each code letter is the file number for the offense.

In each of Questions 33 through 40, the code letters and file numbers should correspond to the capital letters.

If there is an error only in Column 2, mark your answer A.

If there is an error only in Column 3, mark your answer B.

If there is an error in both Column 2 and Column 3, mark your answer C.

If both Columns 2 and 3 are correct, mark your answer D.

Sample Questions:

COLUMN 1	COLUMN 2	COLUMN 3
BNARGHSVVU	emoxtylcci	6357905118

The code letters in Column 2 are correct, but the first 5 in Column 3 should be 2. Therefore, the answer is B.

	COLUMN 1	COLUMN 2	COLUMN 3	
				32.____
33.	HGDSBNBSVR	ytplxmelcx	0945736517	33.____
34.	SDGUUNHVAH	lptiimycoy	5498830120	34.____
35.	BRSNAAVUDU	exlmooctpi	6753221848	35.____
36.	VSRUDNADUS	cleipmopil	1568432485	36.____
37.	NDSHVRBUAG	mplycxeiot	3450175829	37.____
38.	GHUSNVBRDA	tyilmcexpo	9085316742	38.____
39.	DBSHVURANG	pesycixomt	4650187239	39.____
40.	RHNNASBDGU	xymnolepti	7033256398	40.____

KEY (CORRECT ANSWERS)

1.	B	11.	B	21.	D	31.	D
2.	A	12.	A	22.	D	32.	D
3.	D	13.	C	23.	C	33.	C
4.	B	14.	A	24.	D	34.	D
5.	D	15.	C	25.	A	35.	A
6.	A	16.	D	26.	D	36.	C
7.	D	17.	B	27.	D	37.	B
8.	C	18.	A	28.	C	38.	D
9.	C	19.	B	29.	B	39.	A
10.	B	20.	C	30.	A	40.	C

MAP READING

EXAMINATION SECTION
TEST 1

DIRECTIONS: Each question or incomplete statement is followed by several suggested answers or completions. Select the one that BEST answers the question or completes the statement. *PRINT THE LETTER OF THE CORRECT ANSWER IN THE SPACE AT THE RIGHT.*

Questions 1-3.

DIRECTIONS: Questions 1 through 3 are to be answered SOLELY on the basis of the map which appears on the next page. The flow of traffic is indicated by the arrow. If there is only one arrow shown, then traffic flows only in the direction indicated by the arrow. If there are two arrows shown, then traffic flows in both directions. You must follow the flow of traffic.

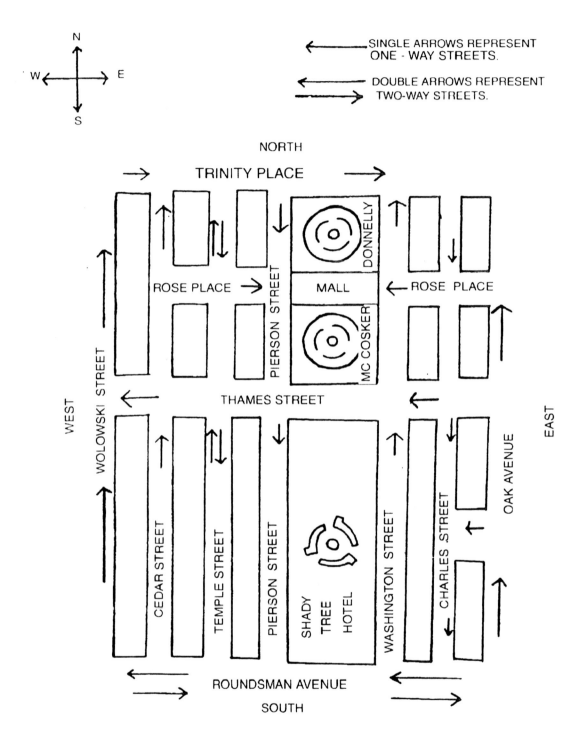

1. Police Officers Simms and O'Brien are located at Roundsman Avenue and Washington   1.____
   Street. The radio dispatcher has assigned them to investigate a motor vehicle accident at
   the corner of Pierson Street and Rose Place.
   Which one of the following is the SHORTEST route for them to take in their patrol car,
   making sure to obey all traffic regulations?
   Travel

   A. west on Roundsman Avenue, then north on Temple Street, then east on Thames
      Street, then north on Pierson Street to Rose Place
   B. east on Roundsman Avenue, then north on Oak Avenue, then west on Rose Place
      to Pierson Street
   C. west on Roundsman Avenue, then north on Temple Street, then east on Rose
      Place to Pierson Street
   D. east on Roundsman Avenue, then north on Oak Avenue, then west on Thames
      Street, then north on Temple Street, then east on Rose Place to Pierson Street

2. Police Officers Sears and Castro are located at Cedar Street and Roundsman Avenue.   2.____
   They are called to respond to the scene of a burglary at Rose Place and Charles Street.
   Which one of the following is the SHORTEST route for them to take in their patrol car,
   making sure to obey all traffic regulations?
   Travel

   A. east on Roundsman Avenue, then north on Oak Avenue, then west on Rose Place
      to Charles Street
   B. east on Roundsman Avenue, then north on Washington Street, then east on Rose
      Place to Charles Street
   C. west on Roundsman Avenue, then north on Wolowski Street, then east on Trinity
      Place, then south on Charles Street to Rose Place
   D. east on Roundsman Avenue, then north on Charles Street to Rose Place

3. Police Officer Glasser is in an unmarked car at the intersection of Rose Place and Tem-   3.____
   ple Street when he begins to follow two robbery suspects. The suspects go south for two
   blocks, then turn left for two blocks, then make another left turn for one more block. The
   suspects realize they are being followed and make a left turn and travel two more blocks
   and then make a right turn.
   In what direction are the suspects now headed?

   A. North   B. South   C. East   D. West

Questions 4-6.

DIRECTIONS: Questions 4 through 6 are to be answered SOLELY on the basis of the follow-
              ing map. The flow of traffic is indicated by the arrows. If there is only one arrow
              shown, then traffic flows only in the direction indicated by the arrow. If there are
              two arrows shown, then traffic flows in both directions. You must follow the flow
              of traffic.

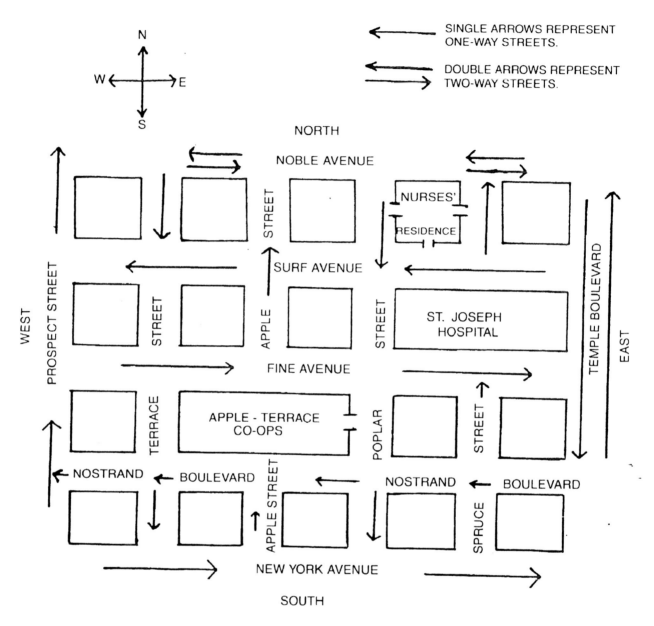

4. Police Officers Gannon and Vine are located at the intersection of Terrace Street and Surf Avenue when they receive a call from the radio dispatcher stating that they need to respond to an attempted murder at Spruce Street and Fine Avenue.
Which one of the following is the SHORTEST route for them to take in their patrol car, making sure to obey all traffic regulations?
Travel _____ to Spruce Street.

    A. west on Surf Avenue, then north on Prospect Street, then east on Noble Avenue, then south on Poplar Street, then east on Fine Avenue
    B. east on Surf Avenue, then south on Poplar Street, then east on Fine Avenue
    C. west on Surf Avenue, then south on Prospect Street, then east on Fine Avenue
    D. south on Terrace Street, then east on Fine Avenue

4.___

5. Police Officers Sears and Ronald are at Nostrand Boulevard and Prospect Street. They receive a call assigning them to investigate a disruptive group of youths at Temple Boulevard and Surf Avenue.
Which one of the following is the SHORTEST route for them to take in their patrol car, making sure to obey all traffic regulations?
Travel

    A. north on Prospect Street, then east on Surf Avenue to Temple Boulevard
    B. north on Prospect Street, then east on Noble Avenue, then south on Temple Boulevard to Surf Avenue
    C. north on Prospect Street, then east on Fine Avenue, then north on Temple Boulevard to Surf Avenue
    D. south on Prospect Street, then east on New York Avenue, then north on Temple Boulevard to Surf Avenue

5.____

6. While on patrol at Prospect Street and New York Avenue, Police Officers Ross and Rock are called to a burglary in progress near the entrance to the Apple-Terrace Co-ops on Poplar Street midway between Fine Avenue and Nostrand Boulevard.
Which one of the following is the SHORTEST route for them to take in their patrol car, making sure to obey all traffic regulations?
Travel _____ Poplar Street.

    A. east on New York Avenue, then north
    B. north on Prospect Avenue, then east on Fine Avenue, then south
    C. north on Prospect Street, then east on Surf Avenue, then south
    D. east on New York Avenue, then north on Temple Boulevard, then west on Surf Avenue, then south

6.____

Questions 7-8.

DIRECTIONS: Questions 7 and 8 are to be answered SOLELY on the basis of the map which appears below. The flow of traffic is indicated by the arrows. If there is only one arrow shown, then traffic flows only in the direction indicated by the arrow. If there are two arrows shown, then traffic flows in both directions. You must follow the flow of traffic.

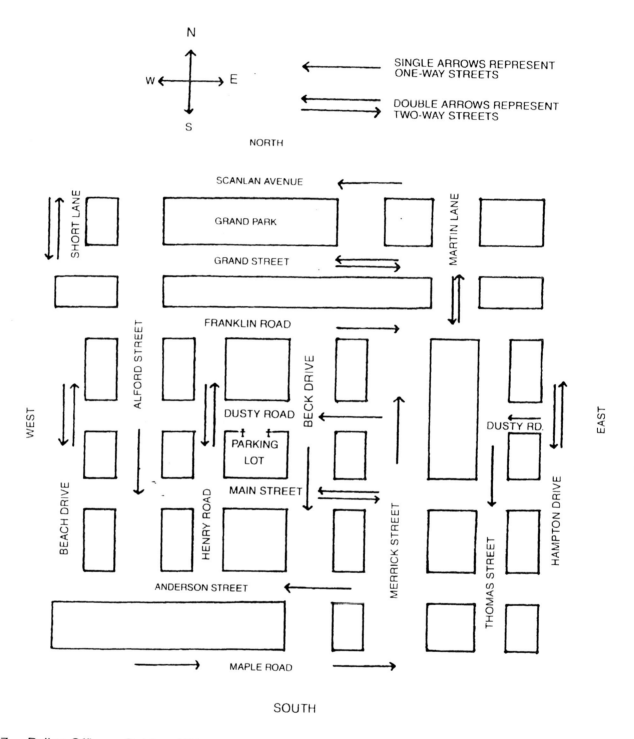

7. Police Officers Gold and Warren are at the intersection of Maple Road and Hampton Drive. The radio dispatcher has assigned them to investigate an attempted auto theft in the parking lot on Dusty Road.
   Which one of the following is the SHORTEST route for the officers to take in their patrol car to get to the entrance of the parking lot on Dusty Road, making sure to obey all traffic regulations?
   Travel _____ to the parking lot entrance.

7.

   A.   north on Hampton Drive, then west on Dusty Road
   B.   west on Maple Road, then north on Beck Drive, then west on Dusty Road
   C.   north on Hampton Drive, then west on Anderson Street, then north on Merrick Street, then west on Dusty Road
   D.   west on Maple Road, then north on Merrick Street, then west on Dusty Road

8.   Police Officer Gladden is in a patrol car at the intersection of Beach Drive and Anderson Street when he spots a suspicious car. Police Officer Gladden calls the radio dispatcher to determine if the vehicle was stolen. Police Officer Gladden then follows the vehicle north on Beach Drive for three blocks, then turns right and proceeds for one block and makes another right. He then follows the vehicle for two blocks, and then they both make a left turn and continue driving. Police Officer Gladden now receives a call from the dispatcher stating the car was reported stolen and signals for the vehicle to pull to the side of the road.
In what direction was Police Officer Gladden heading at the time he signaled for the other car to pull over?

   A.   North   B.   East   C.   South   D.   West

8._____

Questions 9-10.

DIRECTIONS: Questions 9 and 10 are to be answered SOLELY on the basis of the map which appears on the following page. The flow of traffic is indicated by the arrows. If there is only one arrow shown, then traffic flows only in the direction indicated by the arrow. If there are two arrows shown, then traffic flows in both directions. You must follow the flow of traffic.

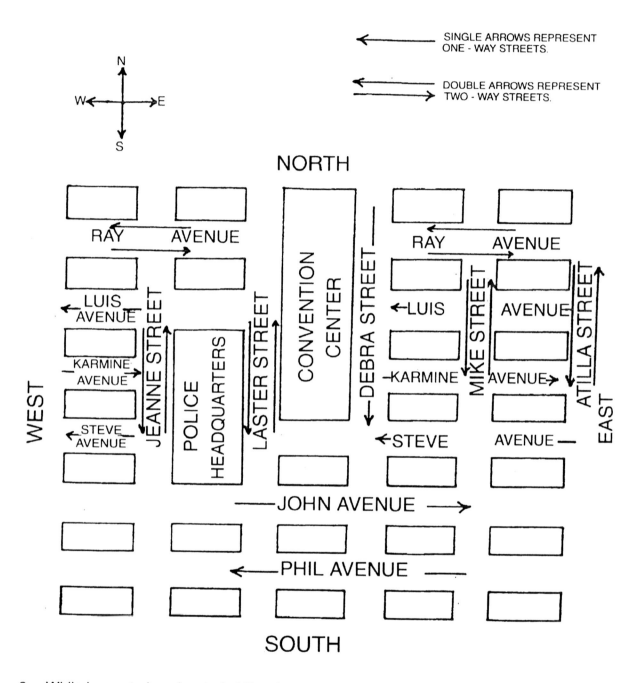

9. While in a patrol car located at Ray Avenue and Atilla Street, Police Officer Ashley receives a call from the dispatcher to respond to an assault at Jeanne Street and Karmine Avenue.

'   Which one of the following is the SHORTEST route for Officer Ashley to follow in his patrol car, making sure to obey all traffic regulations?
Travel

   A. south on Atilla Street, west on Luis Avenue, south on Debra Street, west on Steve Avenue, north on Lester Street, west on Luis Avenue, then one block south on Jeanne Street

   B. south on Atilla Street, then four blocks west on Phil Avenue, then north on Jeanne Street to Karmine Avenue

9.___

    C.   west on Ray Avenue to Debra Street, then five blocks south to Phil Avenue, then west to Jeanne Street, then three blocks north to Karmine Avenue

    D.   south on Atilla Street, then four blocks west on John Avenue, then north on Jeanne Street to Karmine Avenue

10.   After taking a complaint report from the assault victim, Officer Ashley receives a call from the dispatcher to respond to an auto larceny in progress at the corner of Debra Street and Luis Avenue.

    Which one of the following is the SHORTEST route for Officer Ashley to follow in his patrol car, making sure to obey all traffic regulations?
Travel

    A.   south on Jeanne Street to John Avenue, then east three blocks on John Avenue, then north on Mike Street to Luis Avenue, then west to Debra Street

    B.   south on Jeanne Street to John Avenue, then east two blocks on John Avenue, then north on Debra Street to Luis Avenue

    C.   north on Jeanne Street two blocks, then east on Ray Avenue for one block, then south on Lester Street to Steve Avenue, then one block east on Steve Avenue, then north on Debra Street to Luis Avenue

    D.   south on Jeanne Street to John Avenue, then east on John Avenue to Atilla Street, then north three blocks to Luis Avenue, then west to Debra Street

10.____

Questions 11-13.

DIRECTIONS: Questions 11 through 13 are to be answered SOLELY on the basis of the following map. The flow of traffic is indicated by the arrows. You must follow the flow of traffic.

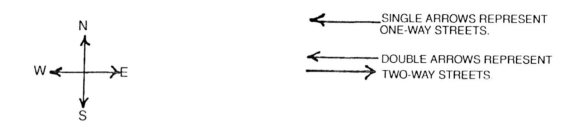

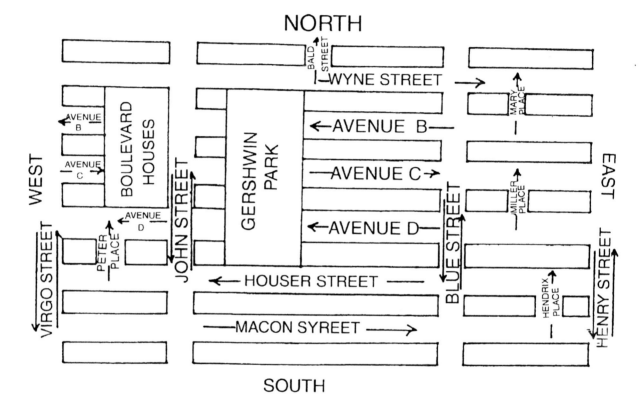

11. Police Officers Ranking and Fish are located at Wyne Street and John Street. The radio   11. ___
dispatcher has assigned them to investigate a motor vehicle accident at the corner of
Henry Street and Houser Street.
Which one of the following is the SHORTEST route for them to take in their patrol car,
making sure to obey all traffic regulations?
Travel

   A. four blocks south on John Street, then three blocks east on Houser Street to Henry
      Street

   B. two blocks east on Wyne Street, then two blocks south on Blue Street, then two
      blocks east on Avenue C, then two blocks south on Henry Street

   C. two blocks east on Wyne Street, then five blocks south on Blue Street, then two
      blocks east on Macon Street, then one block north on Henry Street

   D. five blocks south on John Street, then three blocks east on Macon Street, then one
      block north to Houser Street

12. Police Officers Rizzo and Latimer are located at Avenue B and Virgo Street. They respond to the scene of a robbery at Miller Place and Avenue D.
    Which one of the following is the SHORTEST route for them to take in their patrol car, making sure to obey all traffic regulations?
    Travel _____ to Miller Place.

    A. one block north on Virgo Street, then four blocks east on Wyne Street, then three blocks south on Henry Street, then one block west on Avenue D
    B. four blocks south on Virgo Street, then two blocks east on Macon Street, then two blocks north on Blue Street, then one block east on Avenue D
    C. three blocks south on Virgo Street, then east on Houser Street to Henry Street, then one block north on Henry Street, then one block west on Avenue D
    D. four blocks south on Virgo Street, then four blocks east to Henry Street, then north to Avenue D, then one block west

12._____

13. Police Officer Bendix is in an unmarked patrol car at the intersection of John Street and Macon Street when he begins to follow a robbery suspect. The suspect goes one block east, turns left, travels for three blocks, and then turns right. He drives for two blocks and then makes a right turn. In the middle of the block, the suspect realizes he is being followed and makes a u-turn. In what direction is the suspect now headed?

    A. North   B. South   C. East   D. West

13._____

Questions 14-15.

DIRECTIONS: Questions 14 and 15 are to be answered SOLELY on the basis of the following map. The flow of traffic is indicated by the arrows. If there is only one arrow shown, then traffic flows only in the direction indicated by the arrow. If there are two arrows shown, then traffic flows in both directions. You must follow the flow of traffic.

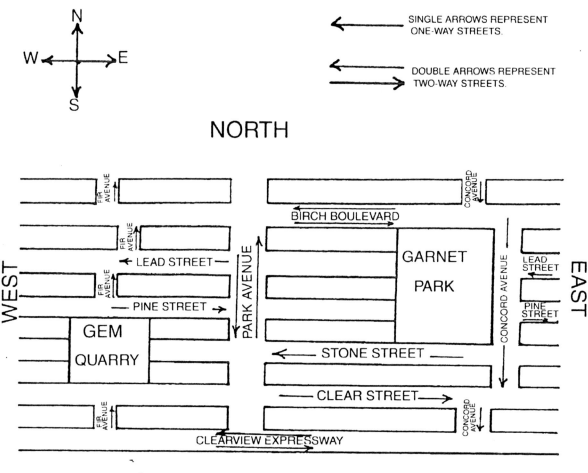

NORTH

SOUTH

14. You are located at Fir Avenue and Birch Boulevard and receive a request to respond to a   14.___
disturbance at Fir Avenue and Clear Street.
Which one of the following is the MOST direct route for you to take in your patrol car,
making sure to obey all traffic regulations?
Travel

    A.   one block east on Birch Boulevard, then four blocks south on Park Avenue, then
one block east on Clear Street

    B.   two blocks east on Birch Boulevard, then three blocks south on Concord Avenue,
then two blocks west on Stone Street, then one block south on Park Avenue, then
one block west on Clear Street

    C.   one block east on Birch Boulevard, then five blocks south on Park Avenue, then
one block west on the Clearview Expressway, then one block north on Fir Avenue

    D.   two blocks south on Fir Avenue, then one block east on Pine Street, then three
blocks south on Park Avenue, then one block east on the Clearview Expressway,
then one block north on Fir Avenue

15. You are located at the Clearview Expressway and Concord Avenue and receive a call to respond to a crime in progress at Concord Avenue and Pine Street. Which one of the following is the MOST direct route for you to take in your patrol car, making sure to obey all traffic regulations?
Travel

    A. two blocks west on the Clearview Expressway, then one block north on Fir Avenue, then one block east on Clear Street, then four blocks north on Park Avenue, then one block east on Birch Boulevard, then two blocks south on Concord Avenue

    B. one block north on Concord Avenue, then one block west on Clear Street, then one block north on Park Avenue, then one block east on Stone Street, then one block north on Concord Avenue

    C. one block west on the Clearview Expressway, then four blocks north on Park Avenue, then one block west on Lead Street, then one block south on Fir Avenue

    D. one block west on the Clearview Expressway, then five blocks north on Park Avenue, then one block east on Birch Boulevard, then two blocks south on Concord Avenue

15.____

Questions 16-20.

DIRECTIONS: Questions 16 through 20 are to be answered SOLELY on the basis of the following map. The flow of traffic is indicated by the arrows. You must follow the flow of traffic.

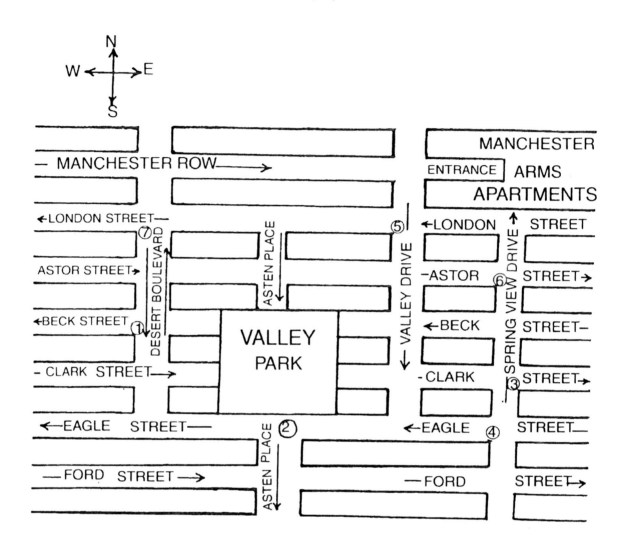

16. If you are located at Point 7 and travel south for one block, then turn east and travel two blocks, then turn south and travel two blocks, then turn east and travel one block, you will be CLOSEST to Point

    A. 2   B. 3   C. 4   D. 6

17. If you are located at Point 3 and travel north for one block, and then turn west and travel one block, and then turn south and travel two blocks, and then turn west and travel one block, you will be CLOSEST to Point

    A. 1   B. 2   C. 4   D. 6

18. You are located at Astor Street and Spring View Drive. You receive a call of a crime in progress at the intersection of Beck Street and Desert Boulevard.
Which one of the following is the MOST direct route for you to take in your patrol car, making sure to obey all traffic regulations?
Travel

    A. one block north on Spring View Drive, then three blocks west on London Street, then two blocks south on Desert Boulevard
    B. three blocks west on Astor Street, then one block south on Desert Boulevard

C. one block south on Spring View Drive, then three blocks west on Beck Street
D. three blocks south on Spring View Drive, then three blocks west on Eagle Street, then two blocks north on Desert Boulevard

19. You are located on Clark Street and Desert Boulevard and must respond to a distur-   19.____
bance at Clark Street and Spring View Drive.
Which one of the following is the MOST direct route for you to take in your patrol car, making sure to obey all traffic regulations?
Travel

   A. two blocks north on Desert Boulevard, then three blocks east on Astor Street, then two blocks south on Spring View Drive
   B. one block south on Desert Boulevard, then three blocks east on Eagle Street, then one block north on Spring View Drive
   C. two blocks north on Desert Boulevard, then two blocks east on Astor Street, then three blocks south on Valley Drive, then one block east on Eagle Street, then one block north on Spring View Drive
   D. two blocks north on Desert Boulevard, then two blocks east on Astor Street, then two blocks south on Valley Drive, then one block east on Clark Street

20. You are located at Valley Drive and Beck Street and receive a call to respond to the cor-   20.____
ner of Asten Place and Astor Street.
Which one of the following is the MOST direct route for you to take in your patrol car, making sure to obey all traffic regulations?
Travel _____ on Astor Street.

   A. one block north on Valley Drive, then one block west
   B. two blocks south on Valley Drive, then one block east on Eagle Street, then three blocks north on Spring View Drive, then two blocks west
   C. two blocks south on Valley Drive, then two blocks west on Eagle Street, then three blocks north on Desert Boulevard, then one block east
   D. one block south on Valley Drive, then one block east on Clark Street, then two blocks north on Spring View Drive, then two blocks west

---

KEY (CORRECT ANSWERS)

1.	C	11.	B
2.	A	12.	A
3.	A	13.	A
4.	D	14.	C
5.	C	15.	D
6.	B	16.	B
7.	C	17.	B
8.	B	18.	A
9.	A	19.	D
10.	A	20.	C

EXAMINATION SECTION
TEST 1

DIRECTIONS: Each question or incomplete statement is followed by several suggested answers or completions. Select the one that BEST answers the question or completes the statement. *PRINT THE LETTER OF THE CORRECT ANSWER IN THE SPACE AT THE RIGHT.*

Questions 1-4.

DIRECTIONS: Questions 1 through 4 are to be answered SOLELY on the basis of the following passage.

Police Officers Ruden and Elliot were on routine patrol on the night of August 21 at 11 P.M. when they were dispatched to the scene of a shooting. They were told to respond to 228 West 64th Street. When they arrived at 11:03 P.M., they saw a man lying in the street in front of 226 West 64th Street. He was bleeding from a gunshot wound to the head. The injured man was identified as Raymond Lopez, a resident of 229 West 64th Street, Apartment 5C. A small crowd gathered along the sidewalk.

An ambulance arrived at 11:06 P.M. Police Officer Keyes helped to put Mr. Lopez into the ambulance, and then accompanied him in the ambulance to try to get more information on the shooting. Two paramedics, John Hayes and Robert Shelton, tried their best to save Mr. Lopez' life but failed. He died at 11:12 P.M. on the way to the hospital. Officer Ruden remained at the scene to get a description of the man who shot Lopez, but witnesses were afraid to talk. Three persons were questioned: Ralph Ricardo, male Hispanic, businessman, age 39, lives at 230 West 64th Street, Apartment 4C; John Fitzpatrick, male White, age 25, cabdriver; and Jimmy Warren, male Black, age 13, who stated that he saw Arthur Gonzalez, the superintendent at 229 West 64th Street, shoot Lopez. Jimmy's mother agreed to let him testify against Gonzalez, who was arrested at 11:29 P.M. on November 25, when he returned to his apartment to get some clothes.

1. Which of the following persons claimed to have seen the shooting?
    A. Ricardo   B. Warren
    C. Lopez   D. Fitzpatrick   1.___

2. When was Gonzalez arrested?
    A. 11:03 P.M., November 24   B. 11:06 P.M., November 25
    C. 11:12 P.M., November 24   D. 11:29 P.M., November 25   2.___

3. The person who was arrested was
    A. a superintendent   B. a cabdriver
    C. a businessman   D. unemployed   3.___

4. Where did the police find Raymond Lopez?   4.___
   _____ West 64th Street.
      A. In Apartment 5C, 228   B. Opposite 229
      C. In Apartment 4C, 230   D. In front of 226

Questions 5-7.

DIRECTIONS: Questions 5 through 7 are to be answered SOLELY on
              the basis of the following passage.

    Police Officers Gillespie and Henderson, working an 8:00 A.M. to
4:00 P.M. shift in the 87th Precinct, receive a radio call to investigate a theft from an automobile at 870 Bayard Street. Officer
Gillespie explains to his partner, who is new to the Precinct, that
the Precinct receives a lot of calls around 9:30 A.M. regarding
thefts from automobiles. This occurs because people come out at
that time to move their cars due to the 10:30 A.M. - 1:30 P.M.
alternate side parking regulation.

    Turning onto Bayard Street, the Officers notice that there are
six automobiles parked on the south side of the street. Officer
Gillespie pulls into a spot behind the last car, in front of 871
Bayard Street, and is greeted by Mrs. Blount. She tells the Officers
that at 9:15 A.M. she discovered that the right front vent window of
her green 1982 Pontiac had been smashed and her car radio worth $500
had been stolen. She mentions that the cars of two of her neighbors,
Mr. Abernathy and Pete Shaw, were also broken into.

    Mr. Abernathy, who lives at 870 Bayard Street, comes out of his
home and walks across the street to speak to the Officers. As Officer
Henderson takes Mrs. Blount's report, Officer Gillespie walks with
Mr. Abernathy to his car to fill out a report. Mr. Abernathy saw a
white male trying to break into his silver gray Le Sabre at 11:05 on
the previous night. Mr. Abernathy called the police, but the officers
who responded were unable to complete the report because they received
a radio call to respond to an assault in progress. Officer Gillespie
takes Mr. Abernathy's report and then rejoins his partner, who is
already completing a report on Pete Shaw's automobile. Having been
on the scene for an hour and ten minutes, they notice it is now
10:50 A.M., and all of the vehicles have been removed, except those
whose owners have just given reports.

5. Officer Henderson completed reports on   5.___
      A. Mrs. Blount and Mr. Abernathy
      B. Mr. Abernathy and Pete Shaw
      C. Mrs. Blount and Pete Shaw
      D. Mr. Abernathy, Pete Shaw, and Mrs. Blount

6. Which side of Bayard Street did Mr. Abernathy live on?   6.___
      A. North   B. South   C. East   D. West

7. When Officers Gillespie and Henderson file the reports,   7.___
   for which person will the date of the crime be different
   from the others?
   A. Mrs. Blount   B. Mr. Abernathy
   C. Mr. Shaw   D. Mr. Blount

Questions 8-12.

DIRECTIONS: Questions 8 through 12 are to be answered SOLELY on
              the basis of the following passage.

   At 2:00 P.M., while sitting in front of 215 Rover Street,
Police Officers Casey and Rogers receive a radio call to investigate
a suspected case of child abuse at 415 Dover Street, Apartment 12B.
The radio dispatcher informs the Officers that the call came from
Apartment 12A. The Officers arrive at the location and decide to
go to the apartment the complaint came from to investigate. When
the Officers knock, both Mr. and Mrs. Fine come to the door. Mrs.
Fine states that she has heard a child crying since noon and asked
her husband to call the police. The Officers thank Mr. and Mrs.
Fine, go on to Apartment 12B, and knock on the door.

   A male named John Brice opens the door and asks what seems to
be the problem. After Officer Casey explains why they are at the
apartment, Mr. Brice states that he works nights and often falls
into a deep sleep. The crying of his child did not awaken him.
Officer Casey asks to see the child, and Mr. Brice complies.
Officer Casey looks at the child and notices bruises and burn marks
on the child's feet. The Officers then request a Patrol Supervisor
and an ambulance. Sergeant Ramos arrives at the apartment at 2:30
P.M. and orders the child removed to a hospital. Fifteen minutes
later, Mr. Brice is arrested. At 3:00 P.M., another patrol car is
sent to notify Mrs. Brice at 725 Clover Street.

8. The police dispatcher received the call from ____ Street,   8.___
   Apartment ____.
   A. 725 Clover; 12C   B. 415 Dover; 12A
   C. 215 Rover; 12B   D. 415 Dover; 12B

9. Who called the police?   9.___
   A. Mrs. Fine   B. Mr. Brice
   C. Mr. Fine   D. Mrs. Brice

10. From which of the following persons did the Officers   10.___
    receive initial information regarding this complaint?
    A. Mrs. Brice   B. Mrs. Fine
    C. Mr. Brice   D. Mr. Fine

11. Mr. and Mrs. Fine called the police because   11.___
    A. the child's crying is disturbing them
    B. Mr. Brice works nights
    C. their child won't stop crying
    D. they suspect child abuse

12. Mrs. Brice   12.___
    A. is notified at 3:00 P.M.
    B. hears a child crying at noon
    C. calls an ambulance at 2:45 P.M.
    D. arrives at the apartment at 2:30 P.M.

Questions 13-15.

DIRECTIONS: Questions 13 through 15 are to be answered SOLELY on
              the basis of the following passage.

Five minutes after the end of his Noon to 1:00 P.M. lunch hour, Police Officer Miller is approached by two obviously frightened teenaged boys. The boys report being robbed by three men while they were listening to music under the boardwalk about twenty minutes earlier.

Danny Brown, the older teenager, informs the Officer that the robbers took his large radio, silver watch, and twenty dollars. His friend, Larry Jones, reports that they took a gold watch and ten dollars from him. The victims report that the perpetrators fled underneath the boardwalk towards the amusement area.

The victims are able to describe the robbers. All three are White males in their late twenties. The first is about 5'6", 160 lbs., wearing white jeans and a blue shirt. The second is about 5'10", 145 lbs., and of dark complexion. The third is known to the younger victim as Redeye and is believed to be a resident of that neighborhood. During the robbery, Redeye was armed with a knife. He is described as being about the same height as the second perpetrator but at least ten pounds heavier than the first. Officer Miller gave the descriptions to the dispatcher.

Officer McMillan, working in the amusement park area, observes three men fitting the description of the robbers. One of the three is carrying a large radio, while the other two are carrying baseball bats and wearing walkman stereos. Officer McMillan quickly requests a police back-up unit to assist in the arrest.

Officers Smith and Campbell respond to provide back-up. Immediately after the three men are apprehended by Officer McMillan and the back-up officers, Officer Miller arrives on the scene accompanied by the victims. The victims identify the three men as the robbers, and the Officers arrest them.

13. What weapon was used in the robbery?   13.___
    A. Baseball bat   B. Knife
    C. Handgun   D. Sword

14. Which one of the following BEST describes Redeye?   14.___
    A. Hispanic, 5'6", dark complexion
    B. White, 5'10", 170 lbs.
    C. Hispanic, 5'6", 160 lbs.
    D. White, 5'10", 155 lbs.

15. Which one of the following Officers was NOT present at   15.___
    the time the suspects were apprehended?
    A. McMillan   B. Campbell   C. Smith   D. Miller

Questions 16-18.

DIRECTIONS: Questions 16 through 18 are to be answered SOLELY on
              the basis of the following passage.

On July 19, while walking home from the subway, Paul Carro was
assaulted by three males on the corner of Evergreen Street and
Appleseed Avenue. Mr. Carro suffered a slight concussion, a broken
nose, and cuts on his face.

When Police Officers James and Blake arrived on the scene, Mr.
Carro was lying on the ground in a semi-conscious state in front of
the subway station. Just as the Officers arrived, a Mrs. Frankel of
1785 Appleseed Avenue, Mr. Jones of 1783 Appleseed Avenue, Ms. Brown
of 851 Evergreen Street, and Mr. Peters of 1787 Appleseed Avenue
came out of their apartments to see what had happened.

Officer James immediately radioed for an ambulance and then
attempted to question Mr. Carro about the incident. Mr. Carro stated
that *there were three young male Whites wearing dungarees, sneakers,
and T-shirts.* Mr. Carro also said that he hit one of the males in
the face and kicked another before he was knocked to the ground.

In the meantime, Officer Blake interviewed the neighbors who
were present. Mr. Jones gave the Officer Mr. Carro's address and
stated that he was Mr. Carro's roommate. He also stated that he
heard a lot of noise on the street; but by the time he came outside,
Mr. Carro was lying on the ground. Both Ms. Brown and Mr. Peters
stated that they saw the three youths who attacked Mr. Carro because
of a remark he made to them. Mr. Peters further stated that Mr.
Carro did not fight back, and at one point said, *Please leave me
alone.* Mrs. Frankel stated that she rushed out of her apartment
just in time to see the young men running off. She said that Mr.
Carro pursued them for a half a block and then collapsed on the
sidewalk. Mrs. Frankel further stated that this was not the first
time that Mr. Carro had started trouble in the neighborhood.

16. Where did Mr. Carro live?   16.___
    A. 1783 Appleseed Avenue   B. 1785 Appleseed Avenue
    C. 851 Evergreen Street   D. 1787 Appleseed Avenue

17. Whose statement to the police directly contradicted Mr.   17.___
    Carro's statement?
    A. Mr. Peters   B. Mr. Jones
    C. Ms. Brown   D. Mrs. Frankel

18. Which one of the following witnesses was the FIRST to be   18.___
    interviewed by Officer Blake?
    A. Mr. Peters   B. Mr. Jones
    C. Ms. Brown   D. Mrs. Frankel

Questions 19-22.

DIRECTIONS: Questions 19 through 22 are to be answered SOLELY on
             the basis of the following passage.

Police Officer Richards, performing an 8:00 A.M. to 4:00 P.M.
tour of duty, is designated as the station house cell block attendant.
During Officer Richards' patrol, he hears moaning sounds coming from
cell block number six, which is occupied by Sam Galvez. Mr. Galvez
is complaining of abdominal pain and requests to go to the hospital.
Officer Richards follows the procedure for a prisoner requiring
medical attention by requesting that an ambulance respond to the
precinct and also notifying the Desk Officer, Lt. Schwinn, who is
talking with Captain Small. When the Emergency Medical Service
attendants arrive, Officer Richards escorts them toward the cell
block. John Ross, a medical attendant, determines after a brief
examination of Mr. Galvez that his pain is probable due to his
appendix.

John Ross and Jack Ryan, the other medical attendant, recommend
that the prisoner be removed to the hospital. Lieutenant Schwinn
assigns Police Officer Ellen Gray to rear handcuff Mr. Galvez and
escort him to the hospital in the ambulance. At the hospital, Mr.
Galvez is seen by Dr. Keegan, the attending physician, who requests
that Officer Gray remove the handcuffs so he may conduct a complete
physical examination. Officer Gray complies with Dr. Keegan's
request. After Dr. Keegan examines the patient, he recommends that
Mr. Galvez be admitted for an appendectomy. Police Officer Gray
notifies the Hospitalized Prisoner Unit at the Court Division,
completes the entries on the Medical Treatment of Prisoners form,
and remains with Mr. Galvez until the arrival of a uniformed Police
Officer, who relieves her.

19. Who assigned Officer Gray to accompany the prisoner?   19.___
    A. Police Officer Richards B. Captain Small
    C. Police Officer Ryan   D. Lieutenant Schwinn

20. The Medical Treatment of Prisoner form was completed by   20.___
    the
    A. escorting officer   B. cell block attendant
    C. Desk Officer   D. medical attendant

21. Prior to examining Mr. Galvez, Dr. Keegan requested that   21.___
    Officer Gray
    A. handcuff Mr. Galvez
    B. leave the examination room
    C. remove the handcuffs from Mr. Galvez
    D. submit a copy of the Medical Treatment form

22. Officer Gray obtained the medical diagnosis from Dr.   22.___
    Keegan and then notified the
    A. Hospitalized Prisoner Unit at the Court Division
    B. Emergency Medical Service attendant, John Ross
    C. Desk Officer, Lieutenant Schwinn
    D. cell block attendant, Police Officer Richards

Questions 23-25.

DIRECTIONS: Questions 23 through 25 are to be answered SOLELY on
              the basis of the following passage.

At 3:55 A.M. on August 3, Police Officer Snow observed four
male Hispanics standing by the emergency exit at the 14th Street
and Union Square subway station. After one of the males spotted
Officer Snow, they all ran down the subway platform. Three of the
males ran out the exit gate and up into the street, while the
fourth male loitered on the platform, stuffing what appeared to be
candy into a paper bag. At 3:57 A.M., Officer Snow stopped and
questioned the male. While Officer Snow was questioning the male,
a call came over her portable radio requesting her to search the
station for unidentified vandals. Officer Snow decided to detain
the male because of the radio call and proceeded to interview the
railroad clerk who had called the police.

At 4:00 A.M., the railroad clerk, Mr. Wallace, stated that four
male Hispanics had broken into the concession stand and removed
several bars of candy, cigarettes, and some cash. Officer Snow
arrested the male she had detained after the railroad clerk identified him as one of the thieves. Officer Snow read the suspect his
constitutional rights at 4:02 A.M., and Sergeant Burns transported
Officer Snow and the suspect to the District 4 office.

The suspect was identified as Louie Rodriguez, of 2948 W. 38th
Street, New York, New York, age seventeen, 5'10", 145 lbs., with
brown eyes and black hair. Officer Snow described one of the other
three suspects as a male Hispanic, approximately 17 to 20 years old,
5'10", slim build, mustache, wearing a black leather jacket, blue
jeans, and white Puma sneakers.

The prisoner was searched by Officer Snow and drugs were found on his person. Lieutenant Nicholson classified the crime as Burglary and Unlawful Possession of a Controlled Substance. Officer Snow entered the crime classification on her arrest forms at 4:54 A.M. and fingerprinted and photographed the prisoner at 5:04 A.M. Officer Snow then called the Warrant Division by telephone to make sure the perpetrator did not have any outstanding warrants. In accordance with procedures, Officer Snow secured the drugs in a sealed envelope containing a serial number.

23. Who transported Officer Snow and the prisoner to the District 4 office?　　　　　　　　　　　　　　　　　　　　　23.___
    A. Lieutenant Nicholson　　B. Lieutenant Wallace
    C. Sergeant Burns　　　　　D. Sergeant Rodriguez

24. What time did Police Officer Snow fingerprint the prisoner?　　　　　　　　　　　　　　　　　　　　　　　　24.___
    _____ A.M.
    A. 3:57　　　　B. 4:02　　　　C. 4:54　　　　D. 5:04

25. When Officer Snow first observed the four males, they were standing by the　　　　　　　　　　　　　　　　　25.___
    A. exit gate　　　　　　　B. emergency exit
    C. concession stand　　　 D. token booth

KEY (CORRECT ANSWERS)

1. B		11. C	
2. D		12. D	
3. A		13. B	
4. D		14. B	
5. C		15. D	
6. A		16. A	
7. B		17. A	
8. B		18. B	
9. C		19. D	
10. B		20. A	

21. C
22. A
23. C
24. D
25. B

TEST 2

DIRECTIONS: Each question or incomplete statement is followed by
several suggested answers or completions. Select the
one that BEST answers the question or completes the
statement. *PRINT THE LETTER OF THE CORRECT ANSWER IN
THE SPACE AT THE RIGHT.*

Questions 1-5.

DIRECTIONS: Questions 1 through 5 are to be answered SOLELY on
the basis of the following passage.

Police Officers Murphy, Shield No. 7348, and Dunkin, Shield No.
3329, were assigned to patrol sector E in the 90th Precinct at 3:30
A.M. in patrol car 1749 on October 2, 1993.

Sector E is a residential area of rundown dilapidated houses
where most of the city's poor live. Police Officers Murphy and
Dunkin were traveling south on Jersey Street having a fairly quiet
tour when they heard a woman's scream coming from an alley about
two blocks south on Jersey Street. Police Officer Dunkin looked
at his watch and saw that it was 3:33 A.M. The Police Officers sped
to the area where they believed the scream came from and stopped in
front of 998 Jersey Street, which was an abandoned building commonly
frequented by junkies and derelicts. Police Officer Murphy called
the Police Dispatcher at 3:35 A.M. to inform him that the Police
Officers were investigating screams and requested back-up assistance.
The Police Officers then walked to the side of the building which
forms an alleyway with 994 Jersey Street. Using flashlights, the
Police Officers entered into an alley until they came upon a woman
lying on her stomach. Police Officer Dunkin touched her arm, feeling
for a pulse, when the woman started moaning. At 3:38 A.M., Police
Officer Murphy radioed for an ambulance, while Police Officer Dunkin
aided and gathered information from the victim. The woman told the
Police Officer that her name is Gloria Vargas, age 21, born on
5/15/72, and that she lives at 1023 Jersey Avenue, Apartment 3H,
with her mother and father, Anna and Joseph Vargas, telephone number
784-3942. Ms. Vargas stated that she had been attending a birthday
party for her friend, Jane Colon at 694 Jersey Street, Apartment 6I,
when she decided to leave at around 3:20 A.M. Since she didn't live
far and the night was warm, she decided to walk home against the
wishes of her friends.

She further stated to Police Officer Dunkin that she did not
remember much after that. All she could recall was that she was
four blocks from home when she was hit on the head and then woke up
in the alley with two cops looking down on her and her purse missing.
At 3:45 A.M., Police Officers Vasquez, Shield No. 473, and Booker,
Shield No. 498, arrived in patrol car 1754 and were informed by
Police Officer Dunkin to search the area for any suspicious person

carrying a lady's purple purse. At 3:47 A.M., an ambulance arrived and Paramedics Anders, Shield No. 561, and Hargrove, Shield No. 623, administered first aid and prepared to take Ms. Vargas to Richmond County Hospital. Mrs. Vargas refused to go to the hospital and stated that she wanted to go home so that her parents would not worry. After their attempts to convince Ms. Vargas to go to the hospital failed, Police Officers Murphy and Dunkin called the dispatcher at 4:02 A.M. to report they were escorting Ms. Vargas home. After a search of the area for suspects proved negative, Police Officers Vasquez and Booker reported to the dispatcher that they were resuming patrol at 4:05 A.M.

Police Officers Murphy and Dunkin arrived at the home of Ms. Vargas and saw that she was safely inside before calling the dispatcher at 4:10 A.M. to indicate that they were resuming patrol. The Police Officers completed Crime Report Number 6395 and Aided Report Number 523 at 4:30 A.M.

1. Of the following, what kind of area is Sector E described as? 1.____
    A. Industrial   B. Suburban
    C. Commercial   D. Residential

2. Of the following, what is the number of the radio car used by Police Officers Vasquez and Booker? 2.____
    A. 1745   B. 1754   C. 1574   D. 5417

3. What is the date of birth of Ms. Vargas? 3.____
    A. 5/11/72   B. 5/15/72   C. 5/11/74   D. 5/15/74

4. What other building helped form an alleyway with 998 Jersey Street? 4.____
    ____ Jersey Street.
    A. 994   B. 1023   C. 694   D. 949

5. In what direction were Police Officers Murphy and Dunkin traveling on Jersey Street? 5.____
    A. North   B. East   C. South   D. West

Questions 6-7.

DIRECTIONS: Questions 6 and 7 are to be answered SOLELY on the basis of the following passage.

On Thursday, September 13, at approximately 9:55 P.M., Detective George Smith, Shield #796, was off-duty and visiting his mother at 415 East 106th Street. While looking out of the first floor window of his mother's apartment, he notices a suspicious Black male sitting in a car with the motor running in front of Joe's Pharmacy, located at 430 East 106th Street between Third and Second Avenues. The car was a blue Chevy Vega with New York license plate number L-77985. Detective Smith leaves the apartment and approaches from the opposite side of the street where he observes two men, both Caucasian, in Joe's Pharmacy. One of the men was standing in front of the cash register, while the other man was pointing a gun at the proprietor, who was pinned against the wall. Detective Smith proceeds to a phone booth on the corner of 106th Street and Second Avenue and dials 911 at 10:00 P.M. He informs 911 operator number 372 of the robbery, gives the address of Joe's Pharmacy, and gives the following description of the perpetrators. The first is a male Caucasian, 5'9", 155 lbs., blonde hair, wearing a brown jacket and black pants. The second is a male Caucasian, 6'3", 175 lbs., bald head, wearing a blue navy coat, black pants, and armed with a gun. The third is a Black male, wearing dark clothing and sitting in a blue Chevy Vega, New York license plate number L-77985. Because Detective Smith is not in uniform, he informs the 911 operator that he is wearing a black leather coat and grey pants. Detective Smith requests a back-up unit to respond without lights or siren. He then proceeds to position himself behind a green vehicle parked in front of a closed liquor store opposite Joe's Pharmacy.

Police Officers Brown and Simms respond in Radio Patrol Car #1186 at 10:03 P.M. and park their vehicle on the northwest side of 106th Street on Second Avenue. Approximately at 10:05 P.M., both perpetrators exit from Joe's Pharmacy and run directly to the waiting vehicle which was blocked by a gypsy cab whose owner entered a grocery store. Detective Smith approaches the suspects' vehicle from the rear, and Police Officers Brown and Simms position themselves in view of the suspects and their vehicle, blocking all means of escape. The perpetrators are apprehended, and the property recovered amounts to $1200 in cash and a hand gun. Police Officers Brown and Simms take the perpetrators to the 23rd Precinct for Detective Smith.

Detective Smith enters Joe's Pharmacy, questions Mr. Velez, the proprietor, informs him of the arrest procedure, and explains to him that he is required to appear at the courthouse the following day to press charges.

Detective Smith, the arresting Police Officer, arrives at the 23rd Precinct at 10:55 P.M., finishes his Police Complaint Report at 11:09 P.M., and removes the perpetrators to Central Booking at 11:20 P.M.

6. Where did Police Officers Brown and Simms park their   6.____
   radio patrol car?
   A. Southwest side of 105th Street on Second Avenue
   B. Southwest side of 105th Street on Third Avenue
   C. Northwest side of 106th Street on Second Avenue
   D. Northwest side of 106th Street on Third Avenue

7. Which one of the following is the BEST description of the   7.____
   second perpetrator?
   A. 5'9", 155 lbs., male, white, blond hair
   B. 5'9", 175 lbs., male, white, bald head
   C. 6'3", 155 lbs., male, white, blond hair
   D. 6'3", 175 lbs., male, white, bald head

Questions 8-11.

DIRECTIONS: Questions 8 through 11 are to be answered SOLELY on the basis of the following passage.

Police Officers Larson and Kelly were on patrol in their radio car in the area of the 13th Precinct when they received a dispatch to go to the scene of a robbery in progress. The dispatcher had received a call from a Mr. Morris, the owner of a liquor store located at 1341 3rd Avenue in Manhattan at 8 P.M.

As the Police Officers arrived at the scene approximately five minutes later, a red Buick was pulling away from the liquor store, and Police Officer Kelly made a note of the license plate number, 346-BYI. They entered the store to find Mr. Morris standing beside an empty cash register. He said that one of the robbers was a White male about 5'10" tall, approximately 180 lbs., blond hair, clean-shaven, wearing a plaid shirt, blue dungarees, and sunglasses. He described the other person as a Black female about 5'6" tall, about 140 lbs., black hair, also wearing dark glasses. She was dressed in a red T-shirt and blue dungarees. The Police Officers asked Mr. Morris to describe what had happened. He stated that a female customer, someone he had never seen before, had just purchased some liquor. The woman asked him where the Peter Cooper apartment complex was located. Mr. Morris gave her directions, and the woman left the store at approximately 7:50 P.M. Almost immediately, the robbers entered the store, and the male drew a gun and demanded all the money in the cash register. Mr. Morris opened the register, and the female took all the money, placed it in a large brown bag, and backed toward the door. The male followed closely while holding a light blue bag over the gun. It was then about 7:58 P.M. Mr. Morris ran to the door and saw the robbers get into a blue Chevy Vega, license plate number 574-KJL.

Police Officer Larson asked for a description of the female who had purchased the liquor immediately prior to the hold-up, and Mr. Morris said she was White, about 5'2" tall, 120 lbs., wearing a straw hat, a smock-type of dress, and carrying a large black bag.

8. When did Mr. Morris report the robbery?   8.____
    _____ P.M.
      A. 7:50   B. 7:58   C. 8:00   D. 8:05

9. The person who drew the gun on the store owner was a   9.____
      A. White male   B. Black female
      C. White female   D. Black male

10. Which one of the following BEST describes the clothing   10.____
    worn by the female robber?
      A. Plaid shirt, blue dungarees
      B. Blue dungarees, blue T-shirt
      C. Smock-type dress and straw hat
      D. Red T-shirt, blue dungarees

11. Which one of the following is the CORRECT license plate   11.___
    number of the car that the Police Officers saw pulling
    away from the liquor store?
       A. 346-BIY   B. 574-KJL   C. 346-BYI   D. 574-KLJ

Questions 12-14.

DIRECTIONS: Questions 12 through 14 are to be answered SOLELY on
               the basis of the following passage.

On Monday evening, February 6, 1994, while I was on duty in the
guard box outside the Liberian Embassy on Lexington Avenue and 38th
Street, I noticed a grey Volvo, New York license plate number 846 DSB,
parked across the street on the northeast corner of 38th Street at
approximately 5:15 P.M. There were two occupants in the car. One
was a White male who had grey hair and was wearing a pale blue
jacket; the other was a young male with a dark complexion who was
wearing a hat, sunglasses, and a dark grey jacket.

After about 20 minutes, the man wearing the dark grey jacket got
out of the car and read the traffic sign which described the parking
regulations. He then spoke to the driver of the car, the man wearing
the blue jacket, and walked up 38th Street toward Park Avenue.
Because I know the parking rules of this area and since the car was
not in violation, I ceased to observe it. However, approximately
five minutes later, my attention was drawn to the sight of the male
passenger who had previously left the car to walk up 38th Street.
He now appeared on Lexington Avenue from the southeast corner of 39th
Street and entered a high-rise building located directly opposite
the Embassy. Almost simultaneously, a blue Ford bearing a New Jersey
license plate number 691 ASD, pulled up to the curb in front of the
building, and the driver, a tall White male with blonde hair, who was
wearing a dark blue suit and carrying a briefcase, got out and entered
the lobby.

I walked across the street from the guard box and went into the
lobby of the high-rise building where the doorman hurried over to
ask if he could assist me. There was no sign of either of the men.
After describing them, I asked the doorman if he knew whether they
were tenants or visitors to the building. He said the tall blonde
man was a tenant by the name of George Altman who lived in Apartment
19G. The other young, dark-complexioned man announced himself as
Mr. Donabuto and entered the elevator with Mr. Altman, whom he had
come to visit. The doorman also added that Mr. Donabuto had visited
the building at least twice the previous week. On one occasion, he
visited Mr. Ehrenwald, a tenant who lives in Apartment 19C. On the
other occasion, he visited Mr. Escobar, who lives in Apartment 19D.
In addition, the doorman said that he had observed Mr. Yepes, the
driver of the grey Volvo, visit Mr. Altman the day before.

After investigating the layout of the building, I decided to
make an entry in the Activity Log and report the incident as suspicious due to the fact that Apartment 19G directly overlooks the
room occupied by the Consul General in the Liberian Embassy.

12. Which one of the following BEST describes the driver of   12.___
    the Volvo?
    A _____ man.
    A. dark-complexioned   B. white, grey-haired
    C. tall blonde   D. dark middle-aged

13. At approximately what time did the young male wearing a   13.___
    hat and sunglasses enter the building on Lexington Avenue?
    _____ P.M.
    A. 5:15   B. 5:20   C. 5:40   D. 6:00

14. At which one of the following locations was the grey   14.___
    Volvo parked?
    _____ corner of _____ Street.
    A. Southeast; 39th   B. Northwest; 39th
    C. Southwest; 38th   D. Northeast; 38th

Questions 15-19.

DIRECTIONS: Questions 15 through 19 are to be answered SOLELY on
                the basis of the following passage.

Police Officer Davies, Shield No. 3935, patrolling Sector D in
the 79th Precinct on Scooter No. 569, was dispatched at 9:26 A.M. on
November 12, 1993 to Roosevelt Houses, 928 Dekalb Avenue, Apartment
15J, on a family dispute. Police Officer Davies requested back-up
units to meet him in front of the building.

Police Officer Davies arrived on the scene at 9:30 A.M. A back-
up unit consisting of Police Officers Mark #2310 and Harris #1542
arrived at the same time in Patrol Car #9843. The Police Officers
were assigned to the same precinct and sector. The Police Officers
took the elevator to the 15th floor and proceeded to Apartment 15J.

The Police Officers rang the apartment bell and were met by a
Black female who told them that she had a court Order of Protection
against her husband. She further stated that her husband was trying
to force his way into the apartment but fled the scene when she
called the police. She gave the following description of her
husband: male, Black, age 38, date of birth 8/14/55, named Carl
Tyler, 6'1" tall, about 185 pounds, clean-shaven, wearing a dark
blue long sleeve shirt, black pants, and black shoes. She further
stated that he resides at 89-27 Bellmore Avenue in Queens, Apartment 2A.

At 9:35 A.M., Police Officers Mark and Harris searched the
building and the surrounding area for Mr. Tyler or for someone fitting the description given by the woman, while Police Officer Davies
obtained further information for his report.

The woman stated her name as Betty Tyler, 37-years-old, born
4/10/56, home telephone number 387-3038. She gave Police Officer
Davies her copy of the Order of Protection, and he recorded the
information in his Memo Book.

The Order of Protection was dated 11/5/93, issued at Brooklyn Criminal Court, 120 Schermerhorn Street, by Judge Harry Cohn, Docket Number APG482/93 and in effect until 1/19/94.

Police Officers Mark and Harris returned to Apartment 5J at 9:45 A.M. after a search for Mr. Tyler proved negative. The Police Officers advised Mrs. Tyler to call the police again if her husband returned.

Police Officers Mark and Harris notified the radio dispatcher that they were resuming patrol at 9:52 A.M. Police Officer Davies proceeded to the station house to prepare two Complaint Reports and to refer the matter to the Detective Unit for follow-up.

15. In which precinct and sector do Police Officer Davies and   15.___
    the back-up Police Officers work?
    _____ Precinct, Sector _____.
        A. 79th; D   B. 79th; B   C. 97th; D   D. 97th; B

16. What is the TOTAL number of Police Officers who responded   16.___
    to assist Police Officer Davies on the family dispute?
        A. 1   B. 2   C. 3   D. 4

17. Which docket number did Police Officer Davies record in   17.___
    his Memo Book?
        A. AFG482/93 B. APG428/93 C. APG482/93 D. AFG428/93

18. Which one of the following is the APPROXIMATE time that   18.___
    Police Officers Mark and Harris arrived at the location?
    _____ A.M.
        A. 9:30   B. 9:35   C. 9:45   D. 9:52

19. Which one of the following is the BEST description of   19.___
    Mr. Tyler?
    Black, 6 ft. _____ in. tall, _____ pounds.
        A. 1; 185   B. 1; 160   C. 6; 185   D. 6; 160

Questions 20-22.

DIRECTIONS: Questions 20 through 22 are to be answered SOLELY on
             the basis of the following passage.

On September 17, 1993, at approximately 11:05 A.M., Police Officers Jesse Harris, Shield #115, and William Anderson, Shield #110, assigned to Radio Patrol Car #9770, received a radio call to respond to a past burglary at 1428 Webster Avenue, Apartment 21B. The Police Officers arrived at the apartment at 11:10 A.M. and were greeted by Mr. George Smith, a Black male, age 61, date of birth 1/10/32. Mr. Smith informed the Police Officers that his apartment had been burglarized.

Mr. Smith told Police Officer Harris that he left his apartment at 9:30 A.M. that morning, 9/17/93, to shop for groceries. Upon his return at approximately 10:45 A.M., he noticed that the cylinder to his apartment lock was removed. Mr. Smith further stated that he did not enter his apartment but asked a neighbor to call the police. Police Officers Harris and Anderson entered the apartment and found only the bedroom ransacked. Police Officer Harris asked Mr. Smith if he noticed any strange or suspicious person on his floor or in the lobby when leaving the building. Mr. Smith reported that he did not notice anyone unusual in the building.

Police Officer Anderson continued the investigation by questioning the tenants who resided on the 21st floor. The tenants questioned were Mrs. Vasques, an Hispanic female, age 40, who lives in Apartment 21E, and Mr. John Fox, a White male, age 32, who lives in Apartment 21F. Police Officer Anderson asked both tenants if they heard or saw anything unusual between the hours of 9:30 A.M. and 10:45 A.M.

At 12:20 P.M., Police Officer Harris notified Police Officer Bell, Shield #169, at the Fingerprint Unit to respond to Mr. Smith's apartment for possible prints. Mr. Smith was informed not to touch anything in the bedroom until the Fingerprint Unit arrived to dust for prints. Police Officer Harris told Mr. Smith to wait until the Fingerprint Unit had completed its work before checking to see what property had been taken. Mr. Smith was told to prepare a list of the missing property and forward it to the precinct.

The Police Officers completed their Police Complaint Report #1010 at 12:40 P.M. and returned to patrol.

20. At what time was the call dispatched to Radio Patrol Car #9770? 20.___
    _____ A.M.
    A. 9:30   B. 10:45   C. 11:05   D. 11:15

21. Which one of the following is Mr. Smith's date of birth? 21.___
    A. 10/10/41   B. 10/10/32   C. 1/10/41   D. 1/10/32

22. How was the apartment entered? 22.___
    A. Door   B. Window   C. Roof   D. Wall

Questions 23-25.

DIRECTIONS: Questions 23 through 25 are to be answered SOLELY on the basis of the following passage.

At 10:30 P.M., Officers Gaines and Palmer respond to a call of shots fired on the fifth floor of a large apartment building. When they arrive on the floor, they are taken to a body of a dead man lying near the stairwell. The man appears to have been shot twice in the head. Officer Gaines remains with the body while Officer Palmer begins interviewing the people standing around the body. The dead man is identified as Charles Morton of Apartment 5C. The interviews reveal the following information:

Mrs. C: About 9:30 P.M., I heard the sounds of an argument coming from next door, Apartment 5C. I recognized one voice as belonging to Mr. Morton. I didn't recognize the other voices, but there were clearly two other men and a woman. I couldn't hear what they were arguing about. At 10:15 P.M., I heard what sounded like two shots coming from that apartment. Then I heard the door slam and people running down the hall. My apartment faces the street so I looked out and about a minute or so later saw two people running out of the building and into a yellow Chevrolet parked in front of this building. Their license plate had all letters on it. I couldn't read the plate numbers. Then I heard someone moaning out in the hall. I opened the door and saw Mr. Morton lying near the steps. Blood was coming from his head. When I got to him, he was dead. Mr. H was standing near him. I then went to my apartment and called the police.

Mr. G: I went to the seven o'clock show at the movies tonight and came back home after the movie. While I was waiting for the elevator, which was on the fifth floor, I noticed that the hall clock said 10:15 P.M. When the elevator arrived, a young man and woman ran out. They seemed to be very excited and nervous. I was curious so I followed them a little and saw them get into a yellow Chevrolet parked in front of this building. I couldn't see the plate that clearly, but it was one of those new plates with all letters on it. They drove up the block and made a right turn at the corner. Then I saw Mr. P arrive from the left with a girl. I went upstairs and saw Mr. Morton's body lying near the fifth floor stairwell. Mr. H was standing next to it.

Mr. P: At 10:30 P.M., my girlfriend and I arrived at this building. I noticed a woman, whom I didn't recognize, quickly getting into a red Chevrolet parked in front of this building. The plate had all letters. The car took off in a real hurry. When we got off at the fifth floor, we saw Mr. Morton lying on the floor with blood pouring from his head. Mr. H and Mrs. S were standing next to the body.

Mr. H: Tonight at 10:00 P.M., after I turned off the TV, I heard noise coming from Mr. Morton's apartment next door. He was arguing with two men, and I heard the word money come up a few times. Anyway, at a quarter after ten, I heard the sound of two gunshots coming from Mr. Morton's apartment. Then the door slammed, and I heard people running down the hall. I heard sounds coming from Mr. Morton's apartment and then from the hall. I opened the door a crack and saw Mr. Morton lying on the floor and pushing himself along. I went out to help him, but I was too late. He said something I couldn't make out, closed his eyes, and died. Mrs. C then came down the hall to the body. She said she was going to call the police.

Mrs. S: I live near the elevator and the stairwell. I heard people running down the hall to the elevator and peeked out of my keyhole. I saw two young men and a woman waiting for the elevator. They seemed nervous. One of the men then took the stairs. About two minutes after the elevator came, I heard moans coming from the hall. I opened my door a crack and saw poor Mr. Morton lying on the carpet dragging himself down the hall. I went to get my keys, locked the door, and went out to see if he needed help. Mr. H was already with him. I just happened to look at my watch and noticed that it was 10:20 P.M.

Mrs. W: About 9:45 P.M., I left my apartment to visit Mrs. L on the second floor and heard a woman and another man arguing with Mr. Morton. Anyway, at 10:15 P.M. when I came back from visiting Mrs. L, I heard three shots ring out. I ran back to my apartment and called the police.

23. Which one of the above people's statements has no bearing   23.___
     on the murder?
         A. Mr. G   B. Mrs. S   C. Mr. P   D. Mrs. W

24. Based on the above information, the Officer should report   24.___
     that there is a conflict in which one of the following
     elements?
     The
         A. identity of the first person to reach the body
         B. location of the murder
         C. location of the get-away car
         D. number of shots fired

25. Based on the above information, the Officer should report   25.___
     that there is a conflict in which one of the following
     elements?
     The
         A. time the shots were fired
         B. number of people heard arguing with Mr. Morton
         C. description of the license plate on the get-away car
         D. location of the body

KEY (CORRECT ANSWERS)

1. D	6. C	11. C	16. B	21. D
2. B	7. D	12. B	17. C	22. A
3. B	8. C	13. C	18. A	23. C
4. A	9. A	14. D	19. A	24. D
5. C	10. D	15. A	20. C	25. B

CODING
EXAMINATION SECTION

COMMENTARY

An ingenious question-type called coding, involving elements of alphabetizing, filing, name and number comparison, and evaluative judgement and application, has currently won wide acceptance in testing circles for measuring clerical aptitude and general ability, particularly on the senior (middle) grades (levels).

While the directions for this question usually vary in detail, the candidate is generally asked to consider groups of names, codes, and numbers, and then, according to a given plan, to arrange codes in alphabetic order; to arrange these in numerical sequence; to re-arrange columns of names and numbers in correct order; to espy errors in coding; to choose the correct coding arrangement in consonance with the given directions and examples, etc.

This question-type appears to have few parameters in respect to form, substance, or degree of difficulty.

Accordingly acquaintance with, and practice in, the coding question is recommended for the serious candidate.

TEST 1

DIRECTIONS: Answer questions 1 through 8 an the basis of the code·table and the instructions given below.

Code Letter for Traffic Problem	B	H	Q	J	F	L	M	I
Code Number for Action Taken	1	2	3	4	5	6	7	8

Assume that each of the capital letters on the above chart is a radio code for a particular traffic problem and that the number immediately below each capital letter is the radio code for the correct action to be taken to deal with the problem. For instance, "1" is the action to be taken to deal with problem "B", "2" is the action to be taken to deal with problem "H", and so forth.

In each question, a series of code letters is given in Column 1. Column 2 gives four different arrangements of code numbers. You are to pick the answer (A, B, C, or D) in Column 2 that gives the code numbers that match the code letters in the same order

SAMPLE QUESTION

Column 1	Column 2
BHLFMQ	A. 125678
	B. 216573
	C. 127653
	D. 126573

According to the chart, the code numbers that correspond to these code letters are as follows: B - 1, M - 2, L- 6, F - 5, M - 7, Q - 3. Therefore, the right answer is 126573. This answer is D in Column 2.

Column 1	Column 2	
1. BHQLMI	A. 123456 B. 123567 C. 123678 D. 125678	1.___
2. HBJQLF	A. 214365 B. 213456 C. 213465 D. 214387	2.___
3. QHMLFJ	A. 321654 B. 345678 C. 327645 D. 327654	3.___
4. FLQJIM	A. 543287 B. 563487 C. 564378 D. 654378	4.___
5. FBIHMJ	A. 518274 B. 152874 C. 528164 D. 517842	5.___
6. MIHFQB	A. 872341 B. 782531 C. 782341 D. 783214	6.___
7. JLFHQIM	A. 465237 B. 456387 C. 4652387 D. 4562387	7.___
8. LBJQIFH	A. 6143852 B. 6134852 C. 61437852 D. 61431852	8.___

KEY (CORRECT ANSWERS)

1.	C	5.	A
2.	A	6.	B
3.	D	7.	C
4.	B	8.	A

TEST 2

DIRECTIONS: Questions 1 through 5 are based on the following list showing the name and number of each of nine inmates.

1. Johnson	4. Thompson	7. Gordon
2. Smith	5. Frank	8. Porter
3. Edwards	6. Murray	9. Lopez

Each question consists of 3 sets of numbers and letters. Each set should consist of the numbers of three inmates and the first letter of each of their names. The letters should be in the same order as the numbers. In at least two of the three choices, there will be an error. On your answer sheet, mark only that choice in which the letters correspond with the numbers and are in the same order. If all three sets are wrong, mark choice D in your answer space.

SAMPLE QUESTION
A.   386 EPM
B.   542 FST
C.   474 LGT

Since 3 corresponds to E for Edwards, 8 corresponds to P for Porter, and 6 corresponds to M for Murray, choice A is correct and should be entered in your answer space. Choice B is wrong because letters T and S have been reversed. Choice C is wrong because the first number, which is 4, does *NOT* correspond with the first letter of choice C, which is L. It should have been T. If choice A were also wrong, then D would be the correct answer.

1. A. 382 EGS	B. 461 TMJ	C. 875 PLF	1.____
2. A. 549 FLT	B. 692 MJS	C. 758 GSP	2.____
3. A. 936 LEM	B. 253 FSE	C. 147 JTL	3.____
4. A. 569 PML	B. 716 GJP	C. 842 PTS	4.____
5. A. 356 FEM	B. 198 JPL	C. 637 MEG	5.____

Questions 6-10

DIRECTIONS: Answer questions 6 through 10 on the basis of the following information:

In order to make sure stock is properly located, incoming units are stored as follows:

STOCK NUMBERS	BIN NUMBERS	
00100 - 39999	D30,	L44
40000 - 69999	I4L,	D38
70000 - 99999	41L,	80D
100000 and over	614,	83D

Using the above table, choose the answer A, B, C, or D, which lists the correct Bin Number for the Stock Number given

6. 17243

    A. 41L   B. 83D   C. I4L   D. D30

7. 9219

    A. D38   B. L44   C. 614   D. 41L

8. 90125

    A. 41L   B. 614   C. D38   D. D30

9. 10001

    A. L44   B. D38   C. 80D   D. 83D

10. 200100

    A. 41L   B. I4L   C. 83D   D. D30

6.___
7.___
8.___
9.___
10.___

KEY (CORRECT ANSWERS)

1. B
2. D
3. A
4. C
5. C

6. D
7. B
8. A
9. A
10. C

TEST 3

DIRECTIONS: Assume that the Police Department is planning to conduct a statistical study of individuals who have been convicted of crimes during a certain year. For the purpose of this study, identification numbers are being assigned to individuals in the following manner:

The first two digits indicate the age of the individual:
The third digit indicates the sex of the individual:
    1.   male
    2.   female

The fourth digit indicates the type of crime involved:
    1.   criminal homicide
    2.   forcible rape
    3.   robbery
    4.   aggravated assault
    5.   burglary
    6.   larceny
    7.   auto theft
    8.   other

The fifth and sixth digits indicate the month in which the conviction occurred:
    01.   January
    02.   February, etc.

Answer questions 1 through 9 *SOLELY* on the basis of the above information and the following list of individuals and identification numbers.

Abbott, Richard	271304	Morris, Chris	212705
Collins, Terry	352111	Owens, William	231412
Elders, Edward	191207	Parker, Leonard	291807
George, Linda	182809	Robinson, Charles	311102
Hill, Leslie	251702	Sands, Jean	202610
Jones , Jackie	301106	Smith, Michael	421308
Lewis, Edith	402406	Turner, Donald	191601
Mack, Helen	332509	White, Barbara	242803

1.   The number of women on the above list is   1.____

   A. 6   B. 7   C. 8   D. 9

2.   The two convictions which occurred during February were for the crimes of   2.____

   A.   aggravated assault and auto theft
   B.   auto theft and criminal homicide
   C.   burglary and larceny
   D.   forcible rape and robbery

3.   The *ONLY* man convicted of auto theft was   3.____

   A.   Richard Abbott   B.   Leslie Hill
   C.   Chris Morris   D.   Leonard Parker

4. The number of people on the list who were 25 years old or older is   4.___

    A. 6   B. 7   C. 8   D. 9

5. The *OLDEST* person on the list is   5.___

    A. Terry Collins   B. Edith Lewis
    C. Helen Mack   D. Michael Smith

6. The two people on the list who are the same age are   6.___

    A. Richard Abbott and Michael Smith
    B. Edward Elders and Donald Turner
    C. Linda George and Helen Mack
    D. Leslie Hill and Charles Robinson

7. A 28-year-old man who was convicted of aggravated assault in October would have identification number   7.___

    A. 281410   B. 281509   C. 282311   D. 282409

8. A 33-year-old woman convicted in April of criminal homicide would have identification number   8.___

    A. 331140   B. 331204   C. 332014   D. 332104

9. The number of people on the above list who were convicted during the first six months of the year is   9.___

    A. 6   B. 7   C. 8   D. 9

Questions 10-19.

DIRECTIONS: The following is a list of patients who were referred by various clinics to the laboratory for tests. After each name is a patient identification number. Answer questions 10 through 19 based on the information contained in this list and the explanation accompanying it.

The *first digit* refers to the clinic which made the referral:

    1. Cardiac   6. Hematology
    2. Renal   7. Gynecology
    3. Pediatrics   8. Neurology
    4. Opthalmology   9. Gastroenterology
    5. Orthopedics

The *second digit* refers to the sex of the patient:

    1. male   2. female

The *third* and *fourth digits* give the age of the patient.

The *last two digits give* the day of the month the laboratory tests were performed.

LABORATORY REFERRALS DURING JANUARY

Adams, Jacqueline	320917	Miller, Michael	511806
Black, Leslie	813406	Pratt, William	214411
Cook, Marie	511616	Rogers, Ellen	722428
Fisher, Pat	914625	Saunders, Sally	310229
Jackson, Lee	923212	Wilson, Jan	416715
James, Linda	624621	Wyatt, Mark	321326
Lane, Arthur	115702		

10. According to the list, the number of women referred to the laboratory during January was   10._____

    A. 4   B. 5   C. 6   D. 7

11. The clinic from which the MOST patients were referred was   11._____

    A. Cardiac   B. Gynecology
    C. Opthamology   D. Pediatrics

12. The YOUNGEST patient referred from any clinic other than Pediatrics was   12._____

    A. Leslie Black   B. Marie Cook
    C. Arthur Lane   D. Sally Saunders

13. The number of patients whose laboratory tests were performed on or before January 16 was   13._____

    A. 7   B. 8   C. 9   D. 10

14. The number of patients referred for laboratory tests who are under age 45 is   14._____

    A. 7   B. 8   C. 9   D. 10

15. The OLDEST patient referred to the clinic during January was   15._____

    A. Jacqueline Adams   B. Linda James
    C. Arthur Lane   D. Jan Wilson

16. The ONLY patient treated in the Orthopedics clinic was   16._____

    A. Marie Cook   B. Pat Fisher
    C. Ellen Rogers   D. Jan Wilson

17. A woman, age 37, was referred from the Hematology clinic to the laboratory. Her laboratory tests were performed on January 9. Her identification number would be   17._____

    A. 610937   B. 623709   C. 613790   D. 623790

18. A man was referred for lab tests from the Orthopedics clinic. He is 30 years old and his tests were performed on January 6. His identification number would be   18._____

    A. 413006   B. 510360   C. 513006   D. 513060

19. A 4 year old boy was referred from Pediatrics clinic to have laboratory tests on January 23. His identification number was   19._____

    A. 310422   B. 310423   C. 310433   D. 320403

KEY (CORRECT ANSWERS)

1.	B		11.	D
2.	B		12.	B
3.	B		13.	A
4.	D		14.	C
5.	D		15.	D
6.	B		16.	A
7.	A		17.	B
8.	D		18.	C
9.	C		19.	B
10.	B			

TEST 4

DIRECTIONS: Questions 1 through 10 are to be answered on the basis of the information and directions given on the following page.

Assume that you are a Senior Stenographer assigned to the personnel bureau of a city agency. Your supervisor has asked you to classify the employees in your agency into the following five groups:

A. employees who are college graduates, who are at least 35 years of age but less than 50, and who have been employed by the. city for five years or more;
B. employees who have been employed by the City for less than five years, who are not college graduates, and who earn at least $32,500 a year but less than $34,500;
C. employees who have been city employees for five years or more, who are at least 21 years of age but less than 35, and who are not college graduates;
D. employees who earn at least $34,500 a year but less than $36,000 who are college graduates, and who have been employed by the city for less than five years;
E. employees who are not included in any of the foregoing groups.

NOTE: In classifying these employees you are to compute age and period of service as of January 1, 2003. In all cases, it is to be assumed that each employee has been employed con-tinuously in City service. In each question, consider only the information which will assist you in classifying each employee. Any information which is of no assistance in classifying an employee should not be considered.

SAMPLE: Mr. Brown, a 29-year-old veteran, was appointed to his present position of Clerk on June 1, 2000. He has completed two years of college. His present salary is $33,050.

The correct answer to this sample is B, since the employee has been employed by the city for less than five years, is not a college graduate, and earns at least $32,500 a year but less than $34,500 .

DIRECTIONS: Questions 1 to 10 contain excerpts from the personnel records of 10 employ-ees in the agency. In the correspondingly numbered space on the right print the capital letter preceding the appropriate group into which you would place each employee,

1. Mr. James has been employed by the city since 1993, when he was graduated from a local college. Now 35 years of age, he earns $36,000 a year.

1._____

2. Mr. Worth began working in city service early in 1999. He was awarded his college degree in 1994, at the age of 21.
As a result of a recent promotion, he now earns $34,500 a year.

2._____

3. Miss Thomas has been a City employee since August 1, 1998. Her salary is $34,500 a year. Miss Thomas, who is 25 years old, has had only three years of high school training.

3._____

4. Mr. Williams has had three promotions since entering city service on January 1, 1991. He was graduated from college with honors in 1974, when he was 20 years of age. His present salary is $37,000 a year.

4._____

5. Miss Jones left college after two years of study to take an appointment to a position in the city service paying $33,300 a year. She began work on March 1, 1997 when she was 19 years of age.

5.___

6. Mr. Smith was graduated from an engineering college with honors in January 1998 and became a city employee three months later. His present yearly salary is $35,810 . Mr. Smith was born in 1976.

6.___

7. Miss Earnest was born on May 31, 1979. Her education consisted of four years of high school and one year of business school. She was appointed as a typist in a city agency on June 1, 1997. Her annual salary is $33,500.

7.___

8. Mr. Adams, a 24-year-old clerk, began his city service on July 1, 1999, soon after being discharged from the U.S.
Army. A college graduate, his present annual salary is $33,200

8.___

9. Miss Charles attends college in the evenings, hoping to obtain her degree in 2004, when she will be 30 years of age. She has been a city employee since April 1998,and earns $33,350.

9.___

10. Mr. Dolan was just promoted to his present position after six years of city service. He was graduated from high school in 1982, when he was 18 years of age, but did not go on to college, Mr. Dolan's present salary is $33,500.

10.___

KEY (CORRECT ANSWERS)

1. A
2. D
3. E
4. A
5. C

6. D
7. C
8. E
9. B
10. E

TEST 5

DIRECTIONS: Questions 1 through 4 each contain five numbers that should be arranged in numerical order. The number with the lowest numerical value should be first and the number with the highest numerical value should be last. Pick that option which indicates the *correct* order of the numbers.

Examples:
A. 9; 18; 14; 15; 27
B. 9; 14; 15; 18; 27
C. 14; 15; 18; 27;   9
D. 9; 14; 15; 27; 18

The correct answer is B, which indicates the proper arrangement of the five numbers.

1. A. 20573; 20753; 20738; 20837; 20098   1._____
    B. 20098; 20753; 20573; 20738; 20837
    C. 20098; 20573; 20753; 20837; 20738
    D. 20098; 20573; 20738; 20753; 20837

2. A. 113492; 113429; 111314; 113114; 131413   2._____
    B. 111314; 113114; 113429; 113492; 131413
    C. 111314; 113429; 113492; 113114; 131413
    D. 111314; 113114; 131413; 113429; 113492

3. A. 1029763; 1030421; 1035681; 1036928; 1067391 3._____
    B. 1030421; 1029763; 1035681; 1067391; 1036928
    C. 1030421; 1035681; 1036928; 1067391; 1029763
    D. 1029763; 1039421; 1035681; 1067391; 1036928

4. A. 1112315; 1112326; 1112337; 1112349; 1112306 4._____
    B. 1112306; 1112315; 1112337; 1112326; 1112349
    C. 1112306; 1112315; 1112326; 1112337; 1112349
    D. 1112306; 1112326; 1112315; 1112337; 1112349

KEY (CORRECT ANSWERS)

1. D
2. B
3. A
4. C

TEST 6

DIRECTIONS: The phonetic filing system is a method of filing names in which the alphabet is reduced to key code letters. The six key letters and their equivalents are as follows:

KEY LETTERS	EQUIVALENTS
b	p, f, v
c	s, k, g, j , q, x, z
d	t
l	none
m	n
r	none

A key letter represents itself.
Vowels (a, e, i, o and u) and the letters w, h, and y are omitted.
For example, the name GILMAN would be represented as follows:

G is represented by the key letter C.
I is a vowel and is omitted.
L is a key letter and represents itself.
M is a key letter and represents itself.
A is a vowel and is omitted.
N is represented by the key letter M.

Therefore, the phonetic filing code for the name GILMAN is CLMM.
Answer questions 1 through 10 based on the information on the previous page.

1. The phonetic filing code for the name FITZGERALD would be

    A. BDCCRLD   B. BDCRLD   C. BDZCRLD   D. BTZCRLD

2. The phonetic filing code CLBR may represent any one of the following names EXCEPT

    A. Calprey   B. Flower   C. Glover   D. Silver

3. The phonetic filing code LDM may represent any one of the following names EXCEPT

    A. Halden   B. Hilton   C. Walton   D. Wilson

4. The phonetic filing code for the name RODRIGUEZ would be

    A. RDRC   B. RDRCC   C. RDRCZ   D. RTRCC

5. The phonetic filing code for the name MAXWELL would be

    A. MCLL   B. MCWL   C. MCWLL   D. MXLL

6. The phonetic filing code for the name ANDERSON would be

    A. AMDRCM   B. ENDRSM   C. MDRCM   D. NDERCN

7. The phonetic filing code for the name SAVITSKY would be

    A. CBDCC   B. CBDCY   C. SBDCC   D. SVDCC

1._

2._

3._

4._

5._

6._

7._

8. The phonetic filing code CMC may represent any one of the following names EXCEPT   8._____

   A. James   B. Jayes   C. Johns   D. Jones

9. The *ONLY* one of the following names that could be represented by the phonetic filing   9._____
   code CDDDM would be

   A. Catalano   B. Chesterton   C. Cittadino   D. Cuttlerman

10. The *ONLY* one of the following names that could be represented by the phonetic filing   10._____
   code LLMCM would be

   A. Ellington   B. Hallerman   C. Inslerman   D. Willingham

———————

KEY (CORRECT ANSWERS)

1. A
2. B
3. D
4. B
5. A

6. C
7. A
8. B
9. C
10. D

———————

NAME AND NUMBER CHECKING
EXAMINATION SECTION
TEST 1

DIRECTIONS: Each question or incomplete statement is followed by several suggested answers or completions. Select the one that *BEST* answers the question or completes the statement. *PRINT THE LETTER OF THE CORRECT ANSWER IN THE SPACE AT THE RIGHT.*

Questions 1-10

DIRECTIONS: Questions 1 through 10 below present the identification numbers, initials, and last names of employees enrolled in a city retirement system. You are to choose the option (A, B, C, or D) that has the *identical* identification number, initials, and last name as those given in each question.

SAMPLE QUESTION

B145698 JL Jones
- A. B146798 JL Jones
- B. B145698 JL Jonas
- C. P145698 JL Jones
- D. B145698 JL Jones

The correct answer is D. Only option D shows the identification number, initials and last name exactly as they are in the sample question. Options A, B, and C have errors in the identification number or last name.

1. J297483 PL Robinson   1.____

    A. J294783 PL Robinson   B. J297483 PL Robinson
    C. J297483 PI Robinson   D. J297843 PL Robinson

2. S497662 JG Schwartz   2.____

    A. S497662 JG Schwarz   B. S497762 JG Schwartz
    C. S497662 JG Schwartz   D. S497663 JG Schwartz

3. G696436 LN Alberton   3.____

    A. G696436 LM Alberton   B. G696436 LN Albertson
    C. G696346 LN Albertson   D. G696436 LN Alberton

4. R774923 AD Aldrich   4.____

    A. R774923 AD Aldrich   B. R744923 AD Aldrich
    C. R774932 AP Aldrich   D. R774932 AD Allrich

5. N239638 RP Hrynyk   5.____

    A. N236938 PR Hrynyk   B. N236938 RP Hrynyk
    C. N239638 PR Hrynyk   D. N239638 RP Hrynyk

6. R156949 LT Carlson   6.____

    A. R156949 LT Carlton   B. R156494 LT Carlson
    C. R159649 LT Carlton   D. R156949 LT Carlson

7. T524697 MN Orenstein   7.____

    A. T524697 MN Orenstein   B. T524967 MN Orinstein
    C. T524697 NM Ornstein   D. T524967 NM Orenstein

8. L346239 JD Remsen   8.____

    A. L346239 JD Remson   B. L364239 JD Remsen
    C. L346329 JD Remsen   D. L346239 JD Remsen

9. P966438 SB Rieperson   9.____

    A. P996438 SB Reiperson   B. P966438 SB Reiperson
    C. R996438 SB Rieperson   D. P966438 SB Rieperson

10. D749382 CD Thompson   10.____

    A. P749382 CD Thompson   B. D749832 CD Thomsonn
    C. D749382 CD Thompson   D. D749823 CD Thomspon

Questions 11 - 20

DIRECTIONS: Each of Questions 11 through 20 gives the identifi-cation number and name of a person who has received treatment at a certain hospital. You are to choose the option (A, B, C, or D) which has *EXACTLY* the same identification number and name as those given in the question.

SAMPLE QUESTION

123765 Frank Y. Jones

    A. 123675 Frank Y. Jones
    B. 123765 Frank T. Jones
    C. 123765 Frank Y. Johns
    D. 123765 Frank Y. Jones

    The correct answer is D. Only option D shows the identification number and name exactly as they are in the sample question. Option A has a mistake in the identification number. Option B has a mistake in the middle initial of the name. Option C has a mistake in the last name.

    Now answer Questions 11 through 20 in the same manner.

11. 754898 Diane Malloy   A. 745898 Diane Malloy   11.__
                                      B. 754898 Dion Malloy
                                      C. 754898 Diane Malloy
                                      D. 754898 Diane Maloy

12. 661818 Ferdinand Figueroa   A. 661818 Ferdinand Figeuroa   12.__
                                        B. 661618 Ferdinand Figueroa
                                        C. 661818 Ferdnand Figueroa
                                        D. 661818 Ferdinand Figueroa

13. 100101 Norman D. Braustein   A. 100101 Norman D. Braustein   13.__
                                        B. 101001 Norman D. Braustein
                                        C. 100101 Norman P. Braustien
                                        D. 100101 Norman D. Bruastein

14. 838696 Robert Kittredge

    A. 838969 Robert Kittredge   14._____
    B. 838696 Robert Kittredge
    C. 388696 Robert Kittredge
    D. 838696 Robert Kittridge

15. 243716 Abraham Soletsky

    A. 243716 Abrahm Soletsky   15._____
    B. 243716 Abraham Solestky
    C. 243176 Abraham Soletsky
    D. 243716 Abraham Soletsky

16. 981121 Phillip M. Maas

    A. 981121 Phillip M. Mass   16._____
    B. 981211 Phillip M. Maas
    C. 981121 Phillip M. Maas
    D. 981121 Phillip N. Maas

17. 786556 George Macalusso

    A. 785656 George Macalusso   17._____
    B. 786556 George Macalusso
    C. 786556 George Maculasso
    D. 786556 George Macluasso

18. 639472 Eugene Weber

    A. 639472 Eugene Weber   18._____
    B. 639472 Eugene Webre
    C. 693472 Eugene Weber
    D. 639742 Eugene Weber

19. 724936 John J. Lomonaco

    A. 724936 John J. Lomanoco   19._____
    B. 724396 John J. Lomonaco
    C. 724936 John J. Lomonaco
    D. 724936 John J. Lamonaco

20. 899868 Michael Schnitzer

    A. 899868 Micheal Schnitzer   20._____
    B. 898968 Michael Schnizter
    C. 899688 Michael Schnitzer
    D. 899868 Michael Schnitzer

Questions: 21 - 28

DIRECTIONS: Questions 21 through 28 consist of lines of names, dates, and numbers which represent the names. membership dates, social security numbers, and members of the retirement system. For each question you are to choose the option (A, B, C, or D) in Column II which *EXACTLY* matches the information in Column I.

SAMPLE QUESTION

Column I

Column II

Crossen 12/23/56 173568929 253492

    A. Crossen 2/23/56 173568929
         253492
    B. Crossen 12/23/56 173568729
         253492
    C. Crossen 12/23/56 173568929
         253492
    D. Crossan 12/23/56 173568929
         258492

The correct answer is C. Only option C shows the name, date, and numbers exactly as they are in Column I. Option A has a mistake in the date. Option B has a mistake in the social security number. Option D has a mistake in the name and in the membership number.

21. Figueroa 1/15/64 119295386 147563   21.___

A.	Figueroa	1/5/64	119295386	147563
B.	Figueroa	1/15/64	119295386	147563
C.	Figueroa	1/15/64	119295836	147563
D.	Figueroa	1/15/64	119295886	147563

22. Goodridge 6/19/59 106237869 128352   22.___

A.	Goodridge	6/19/59	106287869	128332
B.	Goodrigde	6/19/59	106237869	128352
C.	Goodridge	6/9/59	106237869	128352
D.	Goodridge	6/19/59	106237869	128352

23. Balsam 9/13/57 109652382 116938   23.___

A.	Balsan	9/13/57	109652382	116938
B.	Balsam	9/13/57	109652382	116938
C.	Balsom	9/13/57	109652382	116938
D.	Balsalm	9/13/57	109652382	116938

24. Mackenzie 2/16/49 127362513 101917   24.___

A.	Makenzie	2/16/49	127362513	101917
B.	Mackenzie	2/16/49	127362513	101917
C.	Mackenzie	2/16/49	127362513	101977
D.	Mackenzie	2/16/49	127862513	101917

25. Halpern 12/2/73 115206359 286070   25.___

A.	Halpern	12/2/73	115206359	286070
B.	Halpern	12/2/73	113206359	286070
C.	Halpern	12/2/73	115206359	206870
D.	Halpern	12/2/73	115206359	286870

26. Phillips 4/8/66 137125516 192612   26.___

A.	Phillips	4/8/66	137125516	196212
B.	Philipps	4/8/66	137125516	192612
C.	Phillips	4/8/66	137125516	192612
D.	Phillips	4/8/66	137122516	192612

27. Francisce 11/9/63 123926037 152210   27.___

A.	Francisce	11/9/63	123826837	152210
B.	Francisce	11/9/63	123926037	152210
C.	Francisce	11/9/63	123936037	152210
D.	Franscice	11/9/63	123926037	152210

28. Silbert 7/28/54 118421999 178514   28.____

A.	Silbert	7/28/54	118421999	178544
B.	Silbert	7/28/54	184421999	178514
C.	Silbert	7/28/54	118421999	178514
D.	Siblert	7/28/54	118421999	178514

___

KEY (CORRECT ANSWERS)

1.	B		16.	C
2.	C		17.	B
3.	D		18.	A
4.	A		19.	C
5.	D		20.	D
6.	D		21.	B
7.	A		22.	D
8.	D		23.	B
9.	D		24.	B
10.	C		25.	A
11.	C		26.	C
12.	D		27.	B
13.	A		28.	C
14.	B			
15.	D			

TEST 2

Questions 1-3

DIRECTIONS: Items 1 to 3 are a test of your proofreading ability. Each item consists of Copy I and Copy II. You are to assume that Copy I in each item is correct. Copy II, which is meant to be a duplicate of Copy I, may contain some typo-graphical errors. In each item, compare Copy II with Copy I and determine the number of errors in Copy II. If there are:

      no errors, mark your answer A;
      1 or 2 errors, mark your answer B;
      3 or 4 errors, mark your answer C;
      5 or 6 errors, mark your answer D;
      7 errors or more, mark your answer E.

1.   1.___

COPY I

The Commissioner, before issuing any such license, shall cause an investigation to be made of the premises named and described in such application, to determine whether all the provisions of the sanitary code, building code, state industrial code, state minimum wage law, local laws, regulations of municipal agencies, and other requirements of this article are fully observed. (Section B32-169.0 of Article 23.)

COPY II

The Commissioner, before issuing any such license shall cause an investigation to be made of the premises named and described in such applecation, to determine whether all the provisions of the sanitary code, bilding code, state industrial code, state minimum wage laws, local laws, regulations of municipal agencies, and other requirements of this article are fully observed. (Section E32-169.0 of Article 23.)

2.   2.__

COPY I

Among the persons who have been appointed to various agencies are John Queen, 9 West 55th Street, Brooklyn; Joseph Blount, 2497 Durward Road, Bronx: Lawrence K. Eberhardt, 3194 Bedford Street, Manhattan; Reginald L. Darcy, 1476 Allerton Drive, Bronx; and Benjamin Ledwith, 177 Greene Street, Manhattan.

COPY II

Among the persons who have been appointed to various agencies are John Queen, 9 West 56th Street, Brooklyn, Joseph Blount, 2497 Dureward Road, Bronx: Lawrence K. Eberhart , 3194 Belford Street, Manhattan; Reginald L. Barcey, 1476 Allerton drive, Bronx; and Benjamin Ledwith, 177 Green Street, Manhattan.

3.   3._

COPY I

Except as hereinafter provided, it shall be unlawful to use, store or have on hand any inflammable motion picture film in quantities greater than one standard or two sub-stan-dard reels, or aggregating more than two thousand feet in length, or more than ten pounds in weight without the permit required by this section.

COPY II

Except as herinafter provided, it shall be unlawfull to use, store or have on hand any inflamable motion picture film, in quantities greater than one standard or two substandard reels or aggregating more than two thousand feet in length, or more then ten pounds in weight without the permit required by this section.

Questions 4-6

Questions 4 to 6 are a test of your proofreading ability. Each question consists of Copy I and Copy II. You are to assume that Copy I in each question is correct. Copy II, which is meant to be a duplicate of Copy I, may contain some typographical errors. In each question, compare Copy II with Copy I and determine the number of errors in Copy II. If there are

no errors, mark your answer A;
1 or 2 errors, mark your answer B;
3 or 4 errors, mark your answer C;
5 errors or more, mark your answer D.

4.
4.___

COPY I

It shall be unlawful to install wires or appliances for electric light, heat or power, operating at a potential in excess of seven hundred fifty volts, in or on any part of a building, with the exception of a central station, sub-station, transformer, or switching vault, or motor room; provided, however, that the Commissioner may authorize the use of radio transmitting apparatus under special conditions.

COPY II

It shall be unlawful to install wires or appliances for electric light, heat or power, operating at a potential in excess of seven hundred fifty volts, in or on any part of a building, with the exception of a central station, sub-station, transformer, or switching vault, or motor room, provided, however, that the Commissioner may authorize the use of radio transmitting apperatus under special conditions.

5.
5.___

COPY I

The grand total debt service for the fiscal year 2006-07 amounts to $350,563,718.63, as compared with $309,561,347.27 for the current fiscal year, or an increase of $41,002,371.36. The amount payable from other sources in 2006-07 shows an increase of $13,264,165.47, resulting in an increase of $27,733,205.89 payable from tax levy funds.

COPY II

The grand total debt service for the fiscal year 2006-07 amounts to $350,568,718.63, as compared with $309,561,347.27 for the current fiscel year, or an increase of $41,002,371.36. The amount payable from other sources in 2006-07 show an increase of $13,264,165.47 resulting in an increase of $27,733,295.89 payable from tax levy funds.

6.

<u>COPY I</u>

The following site proposed for the new building is approximately rectangular in shape and comprises an entire block, having frontages of about 721 feet on 16th Road, 200 feet on 157th Street, 721 feet on 17th Avenue and 200 feet on 154th Street, with a gross area of about 144,350 square feet. The 2006-07 assessed valuation is $28,700,000 of which $6,000,000 is for improvements.

<u>COPY II</u>

The following site proposed for the new building is approximately rectangular in shape and comprises an entire block, having frontage of about 721 feet on 16th Road, 200 feet on 157th Street, 721 feet on 17th Avenue, and 200 feet on 134th Street, with a gross area of about 114,350 square feet. The 2006-07 assessed valuation is $28,700,000 of which $6,000,000 is for improvements.

———

KEY (CORRECT ANSWERS)

1. D
2. E
3. E
4. B
5. D
6. D

———

TEST 3

Questions 1-8

DIRECTIONS: Each of the Questions numbered 1 through 8 consists of three sets of names and name codes. In each question, the two names and name codes on the same line are supposed to be exactly the same.

Look carefully at each set of names and codes and mark your answer

- A.   if there are mistakes in all three sets
- B.   if there are mistakes in two of the sets
- C.   if there is a mistake in only one set
- D.   if there are no mistakes in any of the sets

SAMPLE QUESTION

The following sample question is given to help you understand the procedure

Macabe, John N. - V 53162	Macade, John N. - V 53162
Howard, Joan S. - J 24791	Howard, Joan S. - J 24791
Ware, Susan B. - A 45068	Ware, Susan B. - A 45968

In the above sample question, the names and name codes of the first set are not exactly the same because of the spelling of the last name (Macabe - Macade). The names and name codes of the second set are exactly the same. The names and name codes of the third set are not exactly the same because the two name codes are different (A 45068 - A 45968). Since there are mistakes in only 2 of the sets, the answer to the sample question is B.

1.   Powell, Michael C. - 78537 F   Powell, Michael C. - 78537 F   1.____
     Martinez, Pablo J. - 24435 P   Martinez, Pablo J. - 24435 P
     MacBane, Eliot M. - 98674 E   MacBane, Eliot M. - 98674 E

2.   Fitz-Kramer Machines Inc.   Fitz-Kramer Machines Inc.   2.____
          - 259090   - 259090
     Marvel Cleaning Service   Marvel Cleaning Service
          - 482657   - 482657
     Donato, Carl G. - 637418   Danato, Carl G. - 687418

3.   Martin Davison Trading Corp.   Martin Davidson Trading Corp.   3.____
          - 43108 T   - 43108 T
     Cotwald Lighting Fixtures   Cotwald Lighting Fixtures
          - 76065 L   - 70056 L
     R. Crawford Plumbers   R. Crawford Plumbers
          - 23157 C   - 23157 G

4. Fraiman Engineering Corp.
        - M4773
    Neuman, Walter B. - N7745
    Pierce, Eric M.   - W6304

    Friaman Engineering Corp.
        - M4773
    Neumen, Walter B. - N7745
    Pierce, Eric M.   - W6304   4.____

5. Constable, Eugene - B 64837
    Derrick, Paul - H 27119
    Heller, Karen - S 49606

    Comstable, Eugene - B 64837
    Derrik, Paul - H 27119
    Heller, Karen - S 46906   5.____

6. Hernando Delivery Service Co.
        - D 7456
    Barettz Electrical Supplies
        - N 5392
    Tanner, Abraham - M 4798

    Hernando Delivery Service Co.
        - D 7456
    Barettz Electrical Supplies
        - N 5392
    Tanner, Abraham - M 4798   6.____

7. Kalin Associates - R 38641
    Sealey, Robert E. - P 63533
    Seals! Office Furniture
        - R 36742

    Kaline Associates - R 38641
    Sealey, Robert E. - P 63553
    Seals! Office Furniture
        - R36742   7.____

8. Janowsky, Philip M.- 742213
    Hansen, Thomas H. - 934816
    L. Lester and Son Inc.
        - 294568

    Janowsky, Philip M.- 742213
    Hanson, Thomas H. - 934816
    L. Lester and Son Inc.
        - 294568   8.____

Questions 9-13

DIRECTIONS: Each of the questions number 9 through 13 consists of three sets of names and building codes. In each question, the two names and building codes on the same line are supposed to be exactly the same.

If you find an error or errors on only *one* of the sets in the question, mark your answer A; any *two* of the sets in the question, mark your answer B; all *three* of the sets in the question, mark your answer C; *none* of the sets in the question, mark your answer D.

Column I
Duvivier, Anne P. - X52714
Dyrborg, Alfred - B4217
Dymnick, JoAnne - P482596

Column II
Duviver, Anne P. - X52714
Dyrborg, Alfred - B4267
Dymnick, JoAnne - P482596

In the above sample question, the first set of names and building codes is not exactly the same because the last names are spelled differently (Duvivier - Duviver). The second set of names and building codes is not exactly the same because the building codes are different (B4217 - B4267). The third set of names and building codes is exactly the same. Since there are mistakes in two of the sets of names and building codes, the answer to the sample question is B.

Now answer the questions on the following page using, the same procedure.

	Column I	Column II	
9.	Lautmann, Gerald G. - C2483 Lawlor, Michael - W44639 Lawrence, John J. - H1358	Lautmann, Gerald C. - C2483 Lawler, Michael - W44639 Lawrence, John J. - H1358	9.____
10.	Mittmann, Howard - J4113 Mitchell, William T.- M75271 Milan, T. Thomas - Q67533	Mittmann, Howard - J4113 Mitchell, William T.- M75271 Milan, T. Thomas - Q67553	10.____
11.	Quarles, Vincent - J34760 Quinn, Alan N. - S38813 Quinones, Peter W. - B87467	Quarles, Vincent - J34760 Quinn, Alan N. - S38813 Quinones, Peter W. - B87467	11.____
12.	Daniels, Harold H. - A26554 Dantzler, Richard - C35780 Davidson, Martina - E62901	Daniels, Harold H - A26544 Dantzler, Richard - 035780 Davidson, Martin - E62901	12.____
13.	Graham, Cecil J. - I20244 Granger, Deborah - T86211 Grant, Charles L. - G5788	Graham, Cecil J. - I20244 Granger, Deborah - T86211 Grant, Charles L. - G5788	13.____

KEY (CORRECT ANSWERS)

1.	D	8.	C
2.	C	9.	B
3.	A	10.	A
4.	B	11.	D
5.	A	12.	C
6.	D	13.	D
7.	B		

TEST 4

Questions 1-9

DIRECTIONS: In questions 1 to 10 there are five pairs of numbers or letters and numbers. Compare each pair and decide how many pairs are *EXACTLY ALIKE*. *PRINT THE LETTER OF THE CORRECT ANSWER IN THE SPACE AT THE RIGHT.*
- A. if only one pair is exactly alike
- B. if only two pairs are exactly alike
- C. if only three pairs are exactly alike
- D. if only four pairs are exactly alike
- E. if all five pairs are exactly alike

1. 73-F......F-73   FF-73. . . .FF-73   1.____
    F-7373....F-7373   373-FF...337-FF
    F-733.....337-F

2. 0-17158. . ..0-17158 0-71518 ... 0-71518   2.____
    0-11758....0-11758   0-15817... 0-15817
    0-51178....0-51178

3. 1A-7908....1A-7908   7A-8901....7A-8091   3.____
    7A-891.....7A-891   1A-9078....1A-9708.
    9A-7018....9A-7081

4. 2V-6426....2V-6246   2N-6246....2N-6246   4.____
    2V-6426....2N-6426   2N-6624....2N-6624
    2V-6462....2V-6462

5. 3NY-56......3ny-65   5NY-356.....3NY-356   5.____
    6NY-3566....3ny-3566 5NY-6536....5NY-6536
    3NY-5663....5ny-3663

6. COB-065....COB-065   BCL-506....BCL-506   6.____
    LBC-650....LBC-650   DLB-560....DLB-560
    CDB-056....COB-065

7. 4KQ-9130....4KQ-9130 4KQ-9310....4KQ-9130   7.____
    4KQ-9031....4KQ-9031 4KQ-9301....4KQ-9301
    4KQ-9013....4KQ-9013

8. MK-89......MK-98   98-MK......89-MK   8.____
    MSK-998........MSK-998 MOSK.......MOKS
    SMK-899....SMK-899

9. 8MD-2104....SMD-2014 2MD-8140....2MD-8140   9.____
    814-MD......814-MD   4MD-8201. . . .4MD-8201
    MD-281......MD-481

10. 161-035. .. .161-035 150-316.... 150-316   10.____
    315-160....315-160   131-650....131-650
    165-301....165-301

──────────

KEY (CORRECT ANSWERS)

1.	B		6.	D
2.	E		7.	D
3.	B		8.	B
4.	C		9.	C
5.	A		10.	E

———

TEST 5

Questions 1-5

DIRECTIONS: Questions 1 through 5, inclusive, consist of groups of four displays representing license identification plates. Examine each group of plates and determine the number of plates in each group which are identical. Mark your answer sheets as follows:

If only two plates are identical, mark answer A.
If only three plates are identical, mark answer B.
If all four plates are identical, mark answer C.
If the plates are all different, mark answer D

EXAMPLE

ABC123   BCD123   ABC123   BCD235

Since only two plates are identical, the first and the third, the correct answer is A.

1. PBV839	PVB839	PVB839	PVB839		1.___
2. WTX083	WTX083	WTX083	WTX083		2.___
3. B73609	D73906	BD7396	BD7906		3.___
4. AK7423	AK7423	AK1423	A81324		4.___
5. 583Y10	683Y10	583Y01	583Y10		5.___

Questions 6-10

DIRECTIONS: Questions 6 through 10 consist of groups of numbers and letters similar to those which might appear on license plates. Each group of numbers and letters will be called a license identification. Choose the license identification lettered A, B, C, or D that *EXACTLY* matches the license identification shown next to the question number.

SAMPLE
NY 1977
ABC-123

A. NY 1976   B. NY 1977   C. NY 1977   D. NY 1977
   ABC-123   ABC-132   CBA-123   ABC-123

The license identification given is NY 1977. The only choice
ABC-123.
that exactly matches it is the license identification next to the letter D. The correct answer is therefore D.

6.   NY 1976   6._____
                           QLT-781

A. NJ 1976   B. NY 1975   C. NY 1976   D. NY 1977
   QLT-781   QLT-781   QLT-781   QLT-781

7.   FLA 1977   7._____
                           2-7LT58J

A. FLA 1977   B. FLA 1977   C. FLA 1977   D. LA 1977
   2-7TL58J   2-7LTJ58   2-7LT58J   2-7LT58J

8.   NY 1975   8._____
                           OQC383

A. NY 1975   B. NY 1975   C. NY 1975   D. NY 1977
   OQC383   OQC833   QCQ383   OCQ383

9.   MASS 1977   9._____
                           B-8DK02

A. MISS 1977 B. MASS 1977 C. MASS 1976 D. MASS 1977
   B-8DK02   B-8DK02   B-8DK02   B-80KD2

10.   NY 1976   10._____
                           ZV0586

A. NY 1976   B. NY 1977   C. NY 1976   D. NY 1976
   2V0586   ZV0586   ZV0586   ZU0586

KEY (CORRECT ANSWERS)

1.	B	6.	C
2.	C	7.	C
3.	D	8.	A
4.	A	9.	B
5.	A	10.	C

TEST 6

DIRECTIONS: Assume that each of the capital letters in the table below represents the name of an employee enrolled in the city employees' retirement system. The number directly beneath the letter represents the agency for which the employee works, and the small letter directly beneath represents the code for the employee's account.

Name of Employee	L	O	T	Q	A	M	R	N	C
Agency	3	4	5	9	8	7	2	1	6
Account Code	r	f	b	i	d	t	g	e	n

In each of the following questions 1 through 3, the agency code numbers and the account code letters in Columns 2 and 3 should correspond to the capital letters in Column 1 and should be in the same consecutive order. For each question, look at each column carefully and mark your answer as follows:

If there are one or more errors *in Column 2 only* , mark your answer A.
If there are one or more errors *in Column 3 only,* mark your answer B.
If there are one or more errors in Column 2 and one or more errors in Column 3, mark your answer C.
If there are *NO* errors in either column, mark your answer D.
The following sample question is given to help you understand the procedure.

Column I	Column 2	Column 3
TQLMOC	583746	birtfn

In Column 2, the second agency code number (corresponding to letter Q) should be "9", not "8". Column 3 is coded correctly to Column 1. Since there is an error only in Column 2, the correct answer is A.

	Column 1	Column 2	Column 3	
1.	Q L N R C A	9 3 1 2 6 8	i r e g n d	1._
2.	N R M O T C	1 2 7 5 4 6	e g f t b n	2._
3.	R C T A L M	2 6 5 8 3 7	g n d b r t	3._

KEY (CORRECT ANSWERS)

1. D
2. C
3. B

POLICE SCIENCE NOTES

POLICE COMMUNICATIONS

Communication can be defined as the transfer of information from one person to another. It can be accomplished in a variety of ways including the spoken word, written message, signal or electrical device. Geographically, communication involves the transmission of messages from one point to another, either interdepartmentally or intradepartmentally. Any exchange of words, messages, or signals in connection with police action may be classified as police communications.

History

Police communications, contrary to many modern beliefs, are as old as the police service itself. In 17th century England, policemen carried bells or lanterns for identification and as signal devices to give warnings or to summon assistance. The 18th century saw little improvement in police signaling equipment. Police officers in the 19th century utilized whistles, night sticks, and even their pistols as signal devices. The 20th century brought the introduction of electrical devices to the field of police communications. The horn, bell, light, telegraph, telephone, radio-telegraph, radio, radar, and now television, afford communications with infinitely increased efficiency. These developments also have produced great strides in the area of speed, range, and area coverage.

Along with these developments in the technical aspects of police communications, the written reporting system of law enforcement agencies have become considerably more sophisticated with the use of automatic and electronic data storage and processing equipment becoming more and more common. This progress has resulted in more accurate, complete, and easily recoverable information for police use.

The rapid growth of police communication probably is the best indication of its success in police administration. It has enabled a remarkable increase in the promptness and effectiveness of police action, especially in emergencies where time is of utmost importance, and closer and more effective control over patrolmen in the field. Most recently developed and available are: two-way radios small enough to be carried on an officer's belt; printout or screen display devices mounted in patrol cars with computer inquiry capability; and automatic query/response devices which show dispatchers or supervisors the geographic locations of patrol cars by radio direction finding systems. Advances in radio communication render perhaps the most important innovations in police methods since the introduction of fingerprinting.

Present Practice

Today's tools of communication are allowing police departments, both large and small, to increase the extent and efficiency of their service. Hardly a single police action is taken that does not involve some sort of communication. Original complaints are usually made to the police department by use of citizen-placed telephone calls. The information is relayed to police dispatchers or other appropriate personnel by use of interoffice phones or by use of mechanical devices, such as the pneumatic tube. In many cases two-way radio is used to relay information to patrol vehicles or to other police departments.

Also helping to stretch the police potential are systems of communication involving teletype, radiotelegraph, land-wire telegraph, long-distance phone circuits, interconnected computer and photo transmitting machines.

These are but a sample of what make up the network of communication found in most police departments. These tools plus proper techniques are invaluable in accomplishing the necessary steps to deal with natural disasters or nuclear attacks. Therefore, knowledge of such tools and techniques are imperative to successful actions of local police auxiliary units.

Telephone Procedures

The citizen's first contact with the police department is often a telephone conversation with an officer. On the telephone you are the police department's voice and whatever you say and how you say it creates for the citizen an impression of the department to that citizen. Every time you pick up the phone you are doing a public relations job. It may be good, bad, or indifferent. Why not always try for the good public relations job?

When considering proper procedures for the use of the telephone, courtesy and consideration are always the keywords. Even when receiving calls from persons who are agitated or excited the proper action remains much the same as in normal telephone calls. Since a large part of police telephone work is receiving calls the following procedures are essential ones.

1. Identify yourself immediately after answering.
2. Speak courteously.
3. Have pad and pencil handy-makes notes when necessary.

On the other hand, when *you* make a call follow the same basic guides of courtesy and consideration. This may be stated as follows:

1. Have in mind what you wish to know or say when your call is answered.

2. Identify yourself and state your business.
3. Have pad and pencil available-make notes when necessary.

Reaching for a telephone is one of our most frequent and familiar gestures. However, this does not guarantee good telephone usage. Proper procedures can result in good telephone usage and are important to proper police work.

Radio Procedure

Two-way radio might well be considered the backbone of police communications. In many instances the proper use of this instrument may well mean the difference between success or failure in any given situation. In general, the same guides apply as did to good telephone procedures, namely, courtesy and consideration. However, a few specific guides are identified for your use.

To transmit a message:
1. Be certain the dispatcher is not busy transmitting other messages.
2. Contact dispatcher, giving your identification, and then wait for dispatcher to answer.
3. Begin your message after the dispatcher has answered you.

While transmitting a message:
1. Speak distinctly into the microphone as in ordinary conversation. Too loud a voice distorts the reception.
2. Speak slowly.
3. Keep messages brief.
4. Mentally rehearse your message before transmitting.
5. Never use vulgar language.

The final rule cannot be overemphasized. Not only is such language in poor taste, but is prohibited by regulations of the FCC. Furthermore, any excess language used, and vulgar language is excess, may well confuse or distort the meaning of your message.

In learning to use radio communications effectively it is necessary to master the codes and specific procedures in effect in your local police department. Appendix II gives some samples of such procedures.

Emergency Information Media

In addition to the telephone and radio communications of the police service, during a CD emergency the auxiliary policeman will need to receive and act on messages disseminated by public information media (radio and television broadcasts, newspapers, etc.) as part of the emergency information program. Although these messages will be intended for the general public, they will also convey information of value to the auxiliary policeman in the performance of his duties. For example, in many local civil defense plans provision is made for certain radio stations to remain on the air as part of the Emergency Broadcasting System, and their broadcasts will convey official information on such matters as warning conditions and last-minute instructions regarding movement to shelters or relocation areas.

ANSWER SHEET

TEST NO. _____ PART _____ TITLE OF POSITION _____

(AS GIVEN IN EXAMINATION ANNOUNCEMENT - INCLUDE OPTION, IF ANY)

PLACE OF EXAMINATION _____ DATE _____

(CITY OR TOWN)   (STATE)

RATING

USE THE SPECIAL PENCIL.   MAKE GLOSSY BLACK MARKS.

	A B C D E		A B C D E		A B C D E		A B C D E		A B C D E
1		26		51		76		101	
2		27		52		77		102	
3		28		53		78		103	
4		29		54		79		104	
5		30		55		80		105	
6		31		56		81		106	
7		32		57		82		107	
8		33		58		83		108	
9		34		59		84		109	
10		35		60		85		110	

Make only ONE mark for each answer.   Additional and stray marks may be
counted as mistakes.   In making corrections, erase errors COMPLETELY.

	A B C D E		A B C D E		A B C D E		A B C D E		A B C D E
11		36		61		86		111	
12		37		62		87		112	
13		38		63		88		113	
14		39		64		89		114	
15		40		65		90		115	
16		41		66		91		116	
17		42		67		92		117	
18		43		68		93		118	
19		44		69		94		119	
20		45		70		95		120	
21		46		71		96		121	
22		47		72		97		122	
23		48		73		98		123	
24		49		74		99		124	
25		50		75		100		125	

34 95

ANSWER SHEET

TEST NO. ______________ PART ______ TITLE OF POSITION ______________________________
(AS GIVEN IN EXAMINATION ANNOUNCEMENT - INCLUDE OPTION, IF ANY)

PLACE OF EXAMINATION ______________________________ (CITY OR TOWN) ______________ (STATE) DATE ______________

RATING

USE THE SPECIAL PENCIL. MAKE GLOSSY BLACK MARKS.

1 A B C D E	26 A B C D E	51 A B C D E	76 A B C D E	101 A B C D E
2 A B C D E	27 A B C D E	52 A B C D E	77 A B C D E	102 A B C D E
3 A B C D E	28 A B C D E	53 A B C D E	78 A B C D E	103 A B C D E
4 A B C D E	29 A B C D E	54 A B C D E	79 A B C D E	104 A B C D E
5 A B C D E	30 A B C D E	55 A B C D E	80 A B C D E	105 A B C D E
6 A B C D E	31 A B C D E	56 A B C D E	81 A B C D E	106 A B C D E
7 A B C D E	32 A B C D E	57 A B C D E	82 A B C D E	107 A B C D E
8 A B C D E	33 A B C D E	58 A B C D E	83 A B C D E	108 A B C D E
9 A B C D E	34 A B C D E	59 A B C D E	84 A B C D E	109 A B C D E
10 A B C D E	35 A B C D E	60 A B C D E	85 A B C D E	110 A B C D E

Make only ONE mark for each answer. Additional and stray marks may be counted as mistakes. In making corrections, erase errors COMPLETELY.

11 A B C D E	36 A B C D E	61 A B C D E	86 A B C D E	111 A B C D E
12 A B C D E	37 A B C D E	62 A B C D E	87 A B C D E	112 A B C D E
13 A B C D E	38 A B C D E	63 A B C D E	88 A B C D E	113 A B C D E
14 A B C D E	39 A B C D E	64 A B C D E	89 A B C D E	114 A B C D E
15 A B C D E	40 A B C D E	65 A B C D E	90 A B C D E	115 A B C D E
16 A B C D E	41 A B C D E	66 A B C D E	91 A B C D E	116 A B C D E
17 A B C D E	42 A B C D E	67 A B C D E	92 A B C D E	117 A B C D E
18 A B C D E	43 A B C D E	68 A B C D E	93 A B C D E	118 A B C D E
19 A B C D E	44 A B C D E	69 A B C D E	94 A B C D E	119 A B C D E
20 A B C D E	45 A B C D E	70 A B C D E	95 A B C D E	120 A B C D E
21 A B C D E	46 A B C D E	71 A B C D E	96 A B C D E	121 A B C D E
22 A B C D E	47 A B C D E	72 A B C D E	97 A B C D E	122 A B C D E
23 A B C D E	48 A B C D E	73 A B C D E	98 A B C D E	123 A B C D E
24 A B C D E	49 A B C D E	74 A B C D E	99 A B C D E	124 A B C D E
25 A B C D E	50 A B C D E	75 A B C D E	100 A B C D E	125 A B C D E